HILDEGARD

OF BINGEN

NEW EDITION

HILDEGARD
OF BINGEN

INSPIRED CONSCIENCE
OF THE TWELFTH CENTURY

RÉGINE PERNOUD

TRANSLATED BY PAUL DUGGAN

MARLOWE & COMPANY
NEW YORK

M38311658

Published by
Marlowe & Company
841 Broadway, Fourth Floor
New York NY 10003

Hildegard of Bingen by Régine Pernoud originally published
in France as *Hildegarde de Bingen, Conscience inspirée du XII siècle* ©
EDITIONS DU ROCHER, nouvelle édition 1995.

This translation by Paul Duggan © 1998
by Marlowe & Company.

Illustrations courtesy of Otto Müller Verlag, Salzburg, Austria, except
"Man at the Center of the Universe" and "St. Hildegard and the Seasons"
courtesy of Scala/Art Resource, NY and "The Human as Microcosm of
the Macrocosm" courtesy of Biblioteca Statale, Lucca, Italy.

Library of Congress Cataloging-in-Publication Data
Pernoud, Régine, 1909–
    [Hildegarde de Bingen. English]
    Hildegard of Bingen : inspired conscience of the twelfth century /
Régine Pernoud. -- New ed.
        p.   cm.
    Includes biographical references.
    ISBN 1-56924-727-7
1. Hildegarde, Saint, 1098–1179. 2. Christian saints--Germany--
Biography.   I. Title.
BX4700.H5P4713 1994
282'.092--dc21   98-4719
[B]   CIP

Manufactured in the United States of America

Contents

AT THE TIME WHEN this work was published, in the autumn of 1994, the musical works of Hildegard of Bingen were beginning to gain surprising favor among the public. Her poems with their melodies—filled both with the "Gregorian" harmony of her times, and with stunning originality—were recorded and achieved unexpected success. So much so that a good number of readers were proving to be curious about the little nun. It had been scarcely fifteen years earlier that we had found her, but since then we had not ceased to do research on her works and to take an interest in her fascinating personality.

In 1982, in fact, *Le Livre des oeuvres divines: Visions* (The Book of Divine Visions) by Hildegard of Bingen was published, presented, and translated by Bernard Gorceix[1]: a most remarkable work, the most penetrating that has appeared in French on the Rhenish abbess. It contains one of the writings of the visionary, preceded by an insightful commentary on the entirety of her work. Regrettably, the author died at the very time of publication, and his death is an irreparable loss for all those interested in the figure of a woman still little-known among us.

[1] Albin Michel, editor.

Nevertheless, this nun from the banks of the Rhine is essential to our knowledge of the twelfth century. Echoing the voice of Saint Bernard, she makes heard a feminine voice, musical in the true sense—the musical part of Hildegard's work is the best known now—of a high order. For she interacted with the most influential people of her age, popes and emperors; in many respects she represents, as Bernard Gorceix stated, the spiritual and political conscience of her times.

Paradoxically, however, it is through her medical works that she is beginning to find public favor today. They are singular works for that era, since they are the only treatises on medicine—or on what we would call the natural sciences—written in the West in the twelfth century: medicine then was practiced instead by the Jewish school in Cordova, that of Maïmonides, taken up in part by Arabs. This is yet another surprising facet of this nun with universal curiosity.

Still, the most fascinating part of her work is really her "cosmic theology," a vision of the universe that is both vast and minute, a dazzling view cast over the world, which the magnificent miniatures of the Lucques manuscript allow us to see in all its brilliance.

This present work, far from being a biography of Hildegard, attempts only to shed light on the different "poles," so to speak, of her thought and activity. Through the study of her correspondence, it concentrates in particular on the sermons that she delivered in several cathedrals, and not the lesser ones: Trier, Cologne, Bamberg, Mainz. . . . For on many occasions she was called upon to preach in public—and the clerics who had listened to her would write to her afterward, asking her to put into writing the sermons she had delivered. This perhaps is the feature that, in our twentieth century, will surprise us the most.

How is it that such an amazing and rich figure has taken so long to be rediscovered—in part—with the attention and interest that she deserves? This makes us put our finger on the lack of intellectual curiosity that our general culture displays. In the United States, in Switzerland, and naturally in Germany, Hildegard of Bingen is well-known today—approached under one aspect or another. We have attempted here to recall some essential features of her work and her person, with the wish that others might be drawn by her as we have been, and that they might approach her works with the breadth needed to make her closer to us, and that a larger public might be able to benefit from everything that she can tell us.

HILDEGARD

OF BINGEN

CHAPTER I

THE WORLD IN 1098

ONE THOUSAND NINETY-EIGHT. A vast tremor runs through the known world, West and East together: this world is on the march, literally. Not in the manner of Caesar in ancient times, when whole armies deployed to watch over the frontiers between Roman and barbarian. No, this time crowds massed at the summons of the pope at the cathedral of Clermont on a wintry Saint Martin's Day, November 18, 1095. Urban II had urged Christians to come to the aid of their brethren in the East and to reconquer Jerusalem, the Holy City.

The waning century had brought only ruinous changes to these Eastern areas. The news came in turn that the holiest of sites, the tomb of Christ, later the place of his Resurrection, the *Anastasis,* had been destroyed at the order of the caliph Hakim: The destruction was started in 1009—on October 18, to be exact, the date carefully noted in Arab chronicles—with the order to leave nothing standing of the rotunda built on the site by the emperor Constantine. Nevertheless Christian pilgrimages to the holy places had not entirely stopped, but had become rarer, and those who returned told about all sorts of horrors of trials and persecutions of which Christians and Jews were victims. Over the years, the situation had only grown worse: The Seljuk Turks, converted to Islam, had overrun Asia Minor and had routed the Byzantine forces who tried to break their thrust at Malazgerd. After that, they fell upon the Armenian population, whom they savagely massacred and whose capital, Ani, they destroyed. The Syrians were treated no better, and the city of Antioch, in spite of its imposing defenses, fell into Turkish hands in 1084. Appeals for help multiplied, issued from the East to Europe across that Mediterranean where the Arab chroniclers complacently repeated that the Westerners could not even "set sail on a plank."

The response to the pope's appeal surpassed all expectations and unleashed throughout Europe a movement of great breadth. There were not just knights and lords, major and minor, "taking up the cross," but also masses of peasants and towndwellers jumping into an adventure whose scope they poorly understood: following some wandering preachers, of whom the most famous in France became known as Peter the Hermit, they left on pilgrimage bearing arms. This was an extraordinary and fatally disorderly drive that could only end in failure, after having advanced and survived by pillage. Nonetheless, one is struck by the organizational spirit shown by the leading lords assigned by their peers to head the movement, as well as by the choice of three different routes to cross Europe, with a general meeting point set at Constantinople. No head of state, king or emperor, set out with his forces; that alone would suffice to differentiate what we have called the Crusades (the term, let us remember, did not appear until the seventeenth century) from the campaigns of conquest that would later take place in Europe.

It was a long march, lasting three years. In 1098, the crusaders arrived outside of the city of Antioch, where, it was said, the surrounding wall had 360 towers. It took them a year of effort, and of countless episodes mingling cunning and courage, to gain control over the city. Beginning in that same year of 1098, the crusaders along their route began to build a cathedral dedicated to Saint Paul at Tarsus, his birthplace. Here we run into another characteristic of that world in turmoil: a passion for building. The city where the council was held, Clermont, held no less than fifty-four churches at the time Pope Urban II was staying there. Moreover, he accomplished a veritable tour of the Romanesque art that was in process of construction, since on the occasion of his journey he went to the dedication of the church of La Chaise-Dieu, and consecrated the high altar of the immense abbey church of Cluny. The latter had just been built, and until the rebuilding of Saint Peter's in Rome in the sixteenth century it remained the largest edifice of Christendom. The pope then went on to consecrate the church of Saint-Flour, the abbatial church of Saint-Géraud d'Aurillac, Saint Stephen's Cathedral in Limoges and the abbey church of Saint-Sauveur in the same city, then the new altars in the Abbey of Saint-Sauveur de Charroux and at the church of Saint-

Hilaire of Poitiers; he also solemnly consecrated the collegiate church of Saint-Sernin of Toulouse, the cathedral of Maguelonne and that of Nîmes, and an altar in the new basilica of Saint-Gilles du Gard—to name only the main stages of this journey where, in our times, the lovers of Romanesque architecture can follow in its tracks. This fervor for building accompanied the expansion of cities in those days; the old cities were expanding, new ones were multiplying, and this would go on for more than two hundred years; the Middle Ages of the châteaux were also that of the cities, to say nothing of the monasteries that were springing up everywhere. The Cluniac reform since the year 910 had been the base for an extraordinary expansion of monastic life. The invasions of the preceding two hundred years had seemed to destroy the very beautiful Christianity of the sixth and seventh centuries, but it was reborn even more beautifully from its ruins. After the reform of Cluny, that of Robert de Molesme, with the foundation of the abbey of Cîteaux precisely in that year of 1098, the observance of the Rule of Saint Benedict went through a deep renewal and enabled prodigious growth of monastic life— with the definitive thrust given shortly afterward by Saint Bernard. The Carthusians, founded by Saint Bruno in 1104, and later the Premonstratensians founded in 1120 at the initiative of Saint Norbert, intensely manifested the spiritual fervor that inspired this amazing epoch.

It is in this world in full flowering that the birth occurred, on a date hard to specify, of a little girl in a family belonging to the local nobility of the Palatinate. Her parents, Hildebert and Matilda (Mechtilde in German) were probably natives of Bermersheim, in the county of Spanheim. She was the couple's tenth child, and received the name Hildegard at baptism. It was an ordinary birth, in a family whose nobility was not marked by grand actions; it was nevertheless a birth that would prove to be in singular accord with the rich and effervescent epoch that was the turn of a century. The following year, on July 15, 1099, the crusaders seized Jerusalem.

A little girl like others. Yet not entirely, since from early childhood she at times astounded those around her. One anecdote narrated later (in the documents of her canonization process) shows her exclaiming to her nursemaid: "See the pretty little calf in that cow. It's white with spots on its brow, on its feet and on its back." When the calf was born some time later, it was clear that it conformed exactly to that description. Hildegard was then five years old. Yet even earlier, she says: "When I was three years old, I saw such a light that my soul was shaken by it; yet because I was a child, I could say nothing about it." She continues:

When I was eight years old, I was offered to God in a spiritual offering and up till age fifteen, I saw many things and I would talk about them sometimes in all simplicity, although those who heard me wondered where it came from and what it was. And I myself was surprised because I would also have outer sight of what I saw with my soul; since I saw that the same did not happen for other people, I concealed as much as I could the vision that I had in my soul. I was unaware of many things in outer life, since I was often sick from the time when my mother suckled me and later. This harmed my development and hindered me in gaining strength.

Hildegard asked her nursemaid whether she also saw what she was seeing. When she answered in the negative, Hildegard was seized with fright and did not dare share with anyone her visions. Still, sometimes during the course of conversation she would speak about events that were going to happen, and when a vision would seize her, she would evoke realities that seemed strange to those listening to her. When the force of her vision would diminish, after it had made her reveal some notions beyond her age, she would feel ashamed of it, would often cry, and keep silent as much as possible. Fearing that those around her would ask her from where this knowledge came to her, she would not dare to say anything more.

One can think that this child with delicate health had a gift of second sight that in its turn amazed and disturbed her family around her. Certain psychologists today acknowledge in children a possibility of intuition superior to that of adults. In Hildegard's case, it seems likely that her family circle had been astounded since her early childhood by her exceptional abilities, and that she herself was troubled by them. In our time, the mother of Thérèse Martin, the little Sister Thérèse of the Infant Jesus, had likewise perceived very early in her daughter a certain predestination.

When Hildegard was eight years old, her parents entrusted her to a young woman of noble birth, Jutta, the daughter of the Count of Spanheim, to educate her. Jutta led the life of a recluse in the monastery of Disibodenberg, not far from Alzey where they lived. She took charge of the little girl who displayed these surprising aptitudes. It was common in those times to entrust a child, boy or girl, to a monastery for education. The one where Jutta of Spanheim had embraced the religious life was a double monastery founded three or four centuries earlier by one of those Irish monks who, following Saint Columban, had left their island literally to sow seeds in Europe, there multiplying their foundations. Some of them, such as that of Saint Gall not far from the Lake of Constance, have survived into our times under different forms. Hildegard would later also write the life of the holy founder Disibod.

Jutta then took into her hands the education of the hardly ordinary girl who had been placed with her. The biographers of Hildegard recount that she taught her the psalms, as well as to play the decachord, the instrument used in accompaniment for singing them. In those days, all education began with song, and by the singing of the psalms; "learning to read" then meant "learning the psalter." It is probable that one would strive to find in the biblical manuscripts the text of the psalms that one had memorized: a kind of global method, since the words themselves were already known, and that reading and writing consisted in finding and then reproducing on tablets the words that the memory had recorded. Hildegard stated later that, although she had learned the text of the psalter, of the Gospel, and of the principal books of the Old and New Testaments, she had not studied the interpretation of the words nor the division of syllables, nor the knowledge of cases and tenses. Jutta had somewhat neglected the teaching of grammar, placing more attention on the texts themselves than on anything else.

The health of her student remained frail. Later her biographer described her in the hagiographical style then in use: "Since vessels of clay are tested in the oven and courage is perfected in infirmity, she did not lack for the sufferings of holiness; these appeared almost from early childhood, and were numerous and nearly continuous, so that she was rarely standing up." She had revealed to Jutta her secret visions. Jutta asked the advice of one of the monks of the monastery of Saint Disibod, Volmar by name; he soon became the counselor, then the assistant and friend of Hildegard, for a period of some thirty years. It was he, also, who acted as her secretary when, as we shall see, the need for this made itself felt.

A sickly and hidden childhood, brightened at times by her visions kept secret, was for Hildegard the beginning of her existence in the context of the double monastery of Disibodenberg, in the Nahe Valley. When she reached the required age, she wanted to take the veil, to become a religious among the women—they seem to have been not very

numerous—who lived in the monastery under Jutta's aegis.
Hildegard would have been then about fourteen or fifteen.
The age of majority was set for girls at twelve (a little later
for boys, at fourteen). As was her childhood, Hildegard's
adolescence was then hidden: as was that of any nun following the Benedictine Rule.

We know rather well how life proceeded for Benedictine
nuns within their convents: their day was marked by the
canonical hours—their day and their night, since, except
for special reasons or health problems, the night was inter-
rupted by the office of matins. These were sung shortly
after midnight. The moment of dawn, that is, as the sun
would rise, was for monks and nuns the time for singing
lauds, which followed the office of prime (the first hour);
the celebration of the Eucharist, the Mass, generally followed, after which breakfast was taken in most convents;
then came the office of terce, the name of which signifies
the third hour after sunrise (eight or nine o'clock, depend-
ing on the season), and a time of work up till the hour of
sext (eleven or twelve o'clock), followed by the meal. Time
was free thereafter up till the hour of none, the ninth hour
(generally two or three o'clock in the afternoon), when
they would resume work, manual or intellectual, collective
or individual; the hour of vespers designated the office of
the end of the day (six or seven o'clock) followed by the
evening meal and by free time, recreation, generally taken
in common. A chapter meeting, all the religious assembled
in the presence of the abbess, would often take place there-

after; after which, as the sun was setting, there was the last singing of the office, that of compline; silence was then to reign in the monastery to allow everyone to rest.

In the course of these different hours, the entire psalter—150 psalms—would be sung within a week's time. Prayer, meditation, work were linked together throughout the day, with the adjustments appropriate to the unfolding of the liturgical year: times of penance such as Lent and Advent; feasts of which the main ones were, as is known, Christmas and Easter; to say nothing of the numerous saints' feasts, the most important one being the feast of the Virgin on February 2, Candlemas, when candles were lit to celebrate the new brightness of Christ, the light of nations, whom his Mother presented in the Temple.

Jutta died in 1136, and it seems that in the meantime the number of nuns gathered around her had increased within the double monastery. They promptly elected Hildegard as abbess. She was soon to turn forty, and did not know that she was approaching the decisive event of her existence, which would engage her on a totally new path.

CHAPTER II

THE REVEALING OF HILDEGARD TO HERSELF AND TO HER CIRCLE

It was in the forty-third year of my temporal course, as I was attracted in great fear to a heavenly vision; while trembling in attention, I saw a very great splendor in which a voice made itself heard from heaven, saying to me, "O frail human, ash from ash, rot from rot, tell and write what you see and hear. But since you are timid in speaking and unskilled in explaining and little taught for writing these things, tell and write, not according to human speech, nor according to the understanding of human invention, nor according to the desire for writing in a human manner, but according to what you see and hear of the heavenly wonders come from God. Repeat them just as they are said to you in the manner of one who listens to the words of a teacher, and present them according to the tenor of the word just as it is intended, as it is made known to you and as it is prescribed to you. Therefore, human, tell what you see and hear. Not in your own manner, nor in the manner of some other human, but according to the will of him who knows, sees and orders everything in the secrecy of his mysteries."

This constitutes a decisive order in which Hildegard's role is specified; she is compared to the prophets of the Old Testament, who are "the mouth of God," transmitting nothing except what they receive, without concern for giving their words the form of a discourse, nor for arranging according to rules of logic or dialectic whatever they must transmit.

Hildegard emphasizes:

And again, I heard a voice from heaven saying to me: "Tell, then, these wonders and write them as they are taught and said to you." This happened in 1141, in the eleven hundred and forty-first year of the Incarnation of Jesus Christ, the Son of God, when I was forty-two years and seven months of age. A light of fire, extremely bright, coming from open sky, poured over my mind totally, over my whole body and my whole chest, as a flame that nonetheless did not burn, but that by its heat inflamed in the manner that the sun heats whatever it shines its rays on.

She continues:

I had felt the power of mysteries, of secrets and of marvelous visions since my youth, namely, since about the time that I was five years old, up till the present, in a wondrous fashion, in myself as at present; still, I had not revealed this to anyone except for a small number of religious people who lived in the same state of life as myself. Otherwise I had kept silence tranquilly the whole time until the moment when God willed for me to make it known by his grace.

She then proceeds to give details about her visions, which we need to examine:

The visions that I have seen occurred not when I was drowsy nor while I was sleeping, nor while in ecstasy, nor by my physical eyes or my outer human ears; I did not perceive them in hidden places. Rather, it is when I am awake that I see them interiorly with my human eyes and ears; simply in the spirit, and I have had them in places uncovered according to God's will.

It is not without hesitation that this kind of message can be accepted. Hildegard shares her anxiety and emphasizes the very distinct—one might even say imperious—character of the order given to her:

How does this happen? It is difficult for a carnal person to know this, but the fact is that, after passing through youth and attaining the maturity when perfect power is gained, I heard a voice from heaven saying: "I am the living Light illuminating whatever is dark. I led wondrously the person whom I wanted, according as he pleased me, into great marvels; I established him above the people of old who were able to see many secrets in me. Yet I cast him down to the ground so that no exaltation of his spirit might arise. The world had in him no joy, nor delight, nor access in those things that properly belonged to him, for I withdrew him from every audacity and stubbornness, leaving him fearful and frightened in suffering. For he suffered in the marrow and the veins of his flesh, with his spirit and senses constrained, and suffering great physical passions so that there was no security remaining in him, but that he could regard himself as guilty in everything that concerned him. For I have enclosed the ruins of his heart of fear so that his spirit might not lift itself up in pride or vainglory, but that he might feel in all these things fears and sufferings, rather than joy and exultation. Therefore, in my love, he has sought in his spirit the one who would open for him the path of salvation. And he found someone and he loved him, recognizing that this was a faithful man and similar to him in that part of the work that concerns me; this, so that my hidden marvels might be revealed. And this same man did not refuse to withdraw to him, but, going to him in the elevation of humility and the intention of the goodwill that he found, he bowed down with many sighs. You, then, O human, who receive what is addressed to you by the manifestation of hidden things, not in the anxiety of deception, but in the purity of a simple spirit, write what you see and hear."

Hildegard continues:

But I, although I saw and heard this, nevertheless, because I doubt and have a bad opinion, and because of the diversity of human words, always, not out of stubbornness, but out of humility, I refused to write until I was forced into the bed of suffering where I lay, stricken by a scourge of God so that I was afflicted by multiple infirmities; I had asked and found, thanks to the witness of a noble girl of high standards and of that man whom I had consulted and found secretly, as I have said, I set my hand to writing. While I was doing this, feeling the great depth of the exposition of the books as I have said, I was relieved of sickness and recovered my strength. With difficulty I have brought this work to an end, dedicating ten years to it. In the days of Henry, archbishop of Mainz, and of Conrad, king of the Romans, and of Cuno, abbot of Saint Disibode, in the times of Pope Eugene, these visions and these words took place. And I have told them and written them, not according to an inquiry of my heart or of any other person, but such as I have seen them in heavenly vision, such as I have heard and perceived the secret mysteries of God. And again, I heard a voice from Heaven saying to me: "Proclaim and write so."

The manner in which the recorded vision is expressed is very surprising for us. For one thing, there is the use of the term *homo,* "man" in the sense of a human creature, a human being. This implies that Hildegard is called really to be a prophet, a mouth of God, repeating the words dictated to her. She would maintain this throughout her life, protesting that she was saying nothing by herself, nothing coming from herself, that she was only repeating and transmitting what "the living Light" was saying to her.

This preface to the first book composed by Hildegard states clearly the new course that her life would take. This turning point is described and dated precisely; she would spend ten years in composing this first work, which she entitled *Scivias—Know the Ways (of the Lord).* The work would then go on from about 1141 until 1151. Yet this was far from being Hildegard's only concern: during that period she would undertake a number of other works, and would begin to manifest the overflow of activity that was characteristic of her.

A certain number of Hildegard's manuscripts are illustrated. Among others, the magnificent volume of her third book preserved in the *Biblioteca governativa* of Lucca contains ten beautiful full-page illustrations reproducing the nun's visions. Below the main image, in a small illuminated box, Hildegard herself is represented, her face lifted toward the image from which flaming streams pour over her. She is sitting on a high-backed chair, before a lectern, holding tablets in her hands; she doubtlessly makes hasty notes on them about the image appearing to her in order to be able to describe it afterward. She is dressed in a black robe covered with a brown mantle, under which can be seen a white tunic of which the sleeves reach down to her wrists, with one hand holding the tablets and the other writing on them. The tablets are of a completely normal form, of black wax, showing two columns each. Facing Hildegard is a monk, seated as she is. He is writing on a parchment codex, and according to the practice of the times he keeps it in place with his ruler while handling his goosefeather quill. This monk, elderly, is very probably Volmar. In some illustrations, particularly in the first miniature of the manuscript of Lucca, behind Hildegard there stands a visibly younger religious, wearing a long black robe, with her head covered by a white coif, from which issues another veil, black also, hanging down her back. This is very probably Richardis, the nun who belonged to the convent of Bingen, about whom Hildegard said that she loved her "as Paul loved Timothy."

This is the image that we will first have of Hildegard. The main part of her life is spent in receiving and transmitting what she calls "the living Light." The monk Volmar, her confessor and probably, through Jutta's mediation, her first confidant, would be her secretary until his own death in 1165. It was through him, no doubt, that the monks of the double monastery of Disibodenberg became informed about the abbess's new activity and about the visions that she was having. This could not fail to disturb ecclesiastical authorities, in this case the abbot himself of the monastery, Cuno; he informed the archbishop of Mainz, Henry, who was in charge of the diocese, about the matter occurring within his purview. Despite surely favorable echoes with regard to the content of these visions, both of them felt somewhat perplexed. It happened that they had just heard toward the end of 1147 that Pope Eugene III would be calling a council in Rheims, and that in preparation for the council he would hold a synod in Trier. At that point, Hildegard's writings consisted of the beginning of her first work, the *Scivias*. This was the chance to submit to the assembled prelates and to the pope himself the work of the visionary religious.

Trier, which people nowadays like to call the oldest city in Germany, was a grand setting for a synod. The *Porta Nigra,* universally known, still attests to the city's age. It is part of the ramparts constructed by the emperor Constantine, who lived in the city until 316 with his mother Helena, who became the Saint Helen of the Christian calendar. Trier was then an important metropolis of the Roman Empire; an active communications node, center of the legions encamped there for containing the barbarian assaults on the border, and a port on the right bank of the Moselle River; it would remain an imperial residence until the end of the fourth century. In the magnificent structure that is the current cathedral, one still discerns the massive plan of the *Dom* erected by Constantine, constituting the core of the edifice. Destroyed on two occasions, by the Franks in the seventh century, and by the Normans at the end of the ninth, it had been rebuilt with the date of 1037. The pope's coming would be an occasion for enlarging it, with a new choir on the eastern side. In this same era Archbishop Hillin would buy back what has always been called the *Aula palatina*, the ancient palace of Constantine that had fallen into ruins, and of which at least a part was restored for receiving the prelates present for the synod.

In order to appreciate the importance of this synod, it is necessary to recall the prolonged discord on Germanic soil between the popes and the emperors; the latter did not resign themselves to abandoning their prerogatives and their customs, acquired during the Carolingian epoch, of intervening in the naming of bishops and of monastery abbots. The reform undertaken by the energetic Gregory VII had only been accepted some twenty years earlier, in

1123, at the time of the agreement that was given the name of the Concordat of Worms. Now, the pope who convened that synod, Eugene III, was a Cistercian trained at Clairvaux by Saint Bernard himself; this meant that this was a pontiff for whom holiness remained the first concern in the exercise of his functions. The council that he would assemble in Rheims would have the object of confirming once again the effort to reform the Church that was evident ever since Gregory VII.

Thus it was an important assembly that gathered in Trier toward the end of 1147. The contrast was striking between the imposing presence of bishops, cardinals, and monastic abbots, presided personally by the pope from Rome—among those present was Bernard of Clairvaux, whose prestige was unchallenged within Christianity and whose influence had been strong enough to calm the troubles provoked by the schism of Anacletus some years earlier—and the slender figure of the little abbess of an obscure convent on the banks of the Rhine, who was said to be favored by divine visions. At the request of Archbishop Henry of Mainz and of Abbot Cuno of Saint Disibode, the pope designated two prelates to go and personally visit Hildegard, to inquire about her conduct, her habits of living, and her writings: the bishop of Verdun, Alberon or Auberon, and his provost Aldebert.

So, both went to Saint Disibode. The inquiry that they conducted was satisfactory, and they brought to Trier the completed part of *Scivias*. An astounding scene followed, which some three hundred years later filled with admiration the abbot of Spanheim, Jean Trithème—a renowned scholar who had gathered more than two thousand manuscripts in his library, and who recounted Hildegard's life after consulting all sources that dealt with her. "The pope," he writes, "read in public, with many people present, the writings of the virgin; he himself performed the office of reader, and set forth a very important part of the work. All those who heard the terms of this reading were filled with admiration and gave thanks together to Almighty God." It was indeed an amazing spectacle that the pope should read before this huge assembly the work of the little religious, until then unknown outside of her immediate circle. The conclusion of all those present has been attributed to Saint Bernard: "Care must be taken not to extinguish so admirable a light moved by divine inspiration."

After the session, Eugene III himself wrote to Hildegard. His letter has been placed at the head of her correspondence, which from then on would constitute an important chapter in the nun's activity. It is the first of a long list: the edition of *Patrologia Latina,* which is not complete, contains 135 letters, each one with its answer, and occupies no less than 240 compactly printed columns in this edition. The pope writes,

We marvel, my daughter, and we marvel beyond what one can believe, that God shows new miracles in our times, as when he pours his Spirit upon you so that it is said of you that you see, understand and explain many secrets. We have learned this from trustworthy persons who tell of having seen and heard you. But what should we say on this matter, we who possess the key of knowledge, in such a way that we can open and close it, and have foolishly neglected to do as much prudently? Thus we wish you well by the grace of God. We wish you well and we address this to your love so that you might know that God resists the proud and gives his grace to the humble [James 4:6]. Thus, preserve and keep this grace that is in you so that you might be aware of what is given to you in spirit, and that you might manifest it in all prudence each time that you hear it. . . . "Open your mouth and I shall fill it [Ps 71]." [At the end Eugene III adds:] What you have told us about the place that you have foreseen in spirit for yourself, let that place be so, with our permission and our blessing, and with that of your bishop, so that there you might live the regular life with your sisters according to the rule of Saint Benedict under the cloister of that place.

Thus did Eugene III express himself in addressing Hildegard. The last sentence needs explanation. In a few words the pope is giving there his approval of the transfer of eighteen nuns grouped around the abbess of the monastery of Saint Disibode over to the place in Bingen that she would make famous. Indeed, for some time it had been evident that the community lacked room in the convent. A new foundation had to be considered. Hildegard had told the abbot and his brothers about the place that, she said, had been shown to her by the Holy Spirit. The place was Rupertsberg, located not far from Saint Disibode—some twenty-five or thirty kilometers—at the confluence of the Rhine and the Nahe Rivers, at Bingerbrück, near the little port of Bingen am Rhein (occupied and fortified at the time of the Roman occupation by Drusus, at the end of the first century B.C.).

This transfer was not achieved without difficulty. The monks of Saint Disibode disapproved of the nuns' leaving, which in fact would diminish their monastery. Hildegard had never seen Rupertsberg where she wished to go; it was a hill that long ago had been named after Saint Robert, the confessor, who had chosen it as his domicile by patrimonial right; he had lived there with his mother Bertha and was buried there. A long conflict ensued, marked by incidents in which the marvelous became mingled with history. Among the monks, a certain Arnold stood out for his vehement opposition to the departure of the nuns, and he stirred up the others to block it. One day he was afflicted by a tumor of the tongue that prevented him from closing his mouth and from talking. Making himself understood through signs, he had himself led to the church of Saint Rupert, where he promised the saint that from then on he would no longer oppose the creation of the monastery, but rather would contribute to it according to his means. He immediately recovered his health, and he was the first to prepare for constructing the buildings, and to uproot the vineyard where the houses were to be put up for accommodating the nuns.

Still, on her part, Hildegard was sick in bed, having lost consciousness and become heavy as a stone. The abbot was told about this; incredulous, he tried both to lift her head and to turn her from one side to another, with no success. Stunned by what the writer of the *Life of Hildegard* calls an "unusual miracle," he comprehended that the will of God was expressing itself there. Abbot Cuno ended by consenting to their departure, which still had to be approved by the canons of the church of Mainz, which they did. Thus "the virgin of the Lord succeeded in coming to live with her sisters in the oratory of Saint Rupert" and in the surrounding dwellings, where the new monastery was created. It was dependent on Count Bernard of Hildesheim, who gave his approval to its establishment. We saw earlier that the project had received approval from the pope himself.

The arrival of the nuns happened in the midst of a crowd of people: Those from Bingen, the neighboring town, rushed over in great jubilation and poured out praises at their coming, while Hildegard and the eighteen religious accompanying her showed their joy and gave thanks to the Lord. The abbess had to be lifted onto a horse and supported from both sides for the entire length of the journey to Rupertsberg. Upon arriving there, she soon regained her strength, and concluded a satisfactory agreement with the brothers of Saint Disibode.

This convent of Rupertsberg, the victim of the Swedish invasions of the seventeenth century, is today a complete ruin. Only the second of the abbess's foundations remains: the convent of Eibingen, located on the right bank of the Rhine in Rüdesheim. It alone survived the destruction by the Swedes, as well as by the French, to which the region fell victim. Several times rebuilt, Hildegard's tomb can be seen there today, as well as the modern mosaics inspired by the nun's visions.

Let us dwell for a while on these predestined places. This is an exceptionally beautiful region, which has always inspired poets, especially the German Romantic movement in the nineteenth century. The two banks of the river from Boppard to Wiesbaden resound with evocative names where all sorts of legends and historical memories cross. The legends are often from a later time, such as that of the *Mäuseturm*, the "mice tower," which stands on a rocky island facing Rupertsberg. The tale is that Hatto, the bishop of Mainz, there had packed reserves of grain in a time of shortages, and, exasperated by the claims and complaints of poor people assailing him, he had them locked in a barn which he set on fire. "Do you hear my mice squeaking?" he asked as he heard their cries. That same night, swarms of mice invaded his palace; he jumped into the Rhine to escape them, but they pursued him and ate him alive. This is a variation of the famous legend of the Pied Piper who led the rats behind him thanks to the magical songs that he played; after he had rid one town of its rodents in this manner, he was refused the payment agreed upon for the task; he came back, and by the music from his flute led the town's children behind him into the river, where they drowned.

On the right bank, a short distance away at Sankt Goarshausen, stands the rock of Lorelei, made famous by Heine's poem. Lorelei is inseparable from the German poetry of the beginning of the nineteenth century. Not far from it is another rock on which legend, as ever, sees the seven girls whom the river god bewitched.

Alongside these pleasant or tragic legends, the vineyards of the Rhine, present everywhere, established the reputation of both the old towns of Lorsch and Rüdesheim, where taverns and open-air cafés still abound today, and which contains a wine museum in a tenth-century fortified castle (Niederbuch). The Benedictine abbey of Eberbach, founded in the twelfth century, a bit farther away at some distance from Wiesbaden, soon became the main wine-growing center of Germany, thanks to the techniques of the Cistercians, who were remarkable experts in every aspect of agriculture in the Middle Ages. The vines in the area are still renowned, while the church, the cloister, and the dormitory, the only vestiges of the abbey, attract only tourists.

Passing nearby Rüdesheim, we take note of the red wines of Assmannshausen, a singularity in the region.

Despite destruction, the region still bristles with towers and castles. At one point, there is a lone clock tower, as in Burg Rheinfels, where it evokes the memory of one of the

strongest fortresses that loomed over the Rhine Valley. At
another, there is another fortified tower, as in Bacharach,
which inspired Guillaume Apollinaire. Modern reconstruc-
tions have often been done of old towers, as in Burg
Sooneck or again, on the right bank, in Burg Lahneck;
also, miraculously, some kilometers from the latter,
Marksburg has come down to us from the thirteenth century and is the only one left intact. There are also some castles and churches, such as Braubach from the thirteenth
century or Oestrich from the twelfth (albeit with a major
restoration during the Renaissance). Thus, over a hundred-
kilometer stretch, the souvenirs of the past weave, in an
atmosphere that is both medieval and romantic, an exceptional setting of art and charm throughout the history of
Saint Hildegard and her companions. This environment
cannot be separated from the works of the visionary: it was
attributed to the grandeur of the one who revealed to her
the living Light dwelling in her.

The installation in Rupertsberg of Hildegard and of the
nuns whose abbess she was is dated around 1148–1150.
She would write the biography of the two saints who
presided over the places where her community was succes-
sively established. Saint Disibode, the Irishman who settled
in the seventh century on the banks of the Rhine with, it is
said, three companions for whom he became abbot while
remaining a hermit, lived apart and did not join his monks
except for reciting the office, up till his death around the

year 700. He thus shared in that kind of immense crusade or migration of Irish people who, during the Middle Ages, left their beloved island out of a spirit of sacrifice in order to go to settle, preferably in deserted places, and to live a contemplative life. Not far from there, Saint Gall founded, in more or less the same period, the monastery that has survived into our own times, near the Lake of Constance. As for Saint Rupert or Robert, he was a Frank, related besides to the great family of Merovingian kings. In 696, he was bishop of Worms; expelled by pagans who were still numerous in that region, he took refuge in Regensburg (Ratisbon). He then founded a community around which a whole city sprang up, the current-day Salzburg. Finally, he returned to die in his diocese of Worms, in 718. It is said that he was buried at Rupertsberg.

These two biographies amount only to a side activity in Hildegard's life, full as it was; nonetheless, they call to mind the establishment of the two successive convents that were the sites of her life, her prayer, and her visions before she founded the third, that of Eibingen near Rüdesheim, this time on the right bank of the Rhine. This last foundation probably dates from 1165.

We must imagine a life at Rupertsberg going on within the context of a monastery that was still under construction, or at least in process of being fitted out, amid the vineyards on the banks of the Rhine, since Hildegard and her companions moved into provisional buildings that would be finished or completed in the years ahead. This is without doubt what is alluded to in a passage from her *Life* (chapter three), in which she recounts that, after a period of illness, she became aware that there was need, "with my spirit comforted, to take care of my daughters both in their corporal needs and in those of their souls, as had been assigned to me by my masters"—this word doubtlessly refers either to her confessor or simply to the Benedictine Rule. Some of the nuns were indeed showing lassitude and discouragement.

I saw in my true vision, with much distress, that the spirits of bronze [evil spirits] were fighting against us. I saw that these same spirits were attacking some of my noble daughters through various vanities and were keeping them ensnared. Then, taught by God, I taught them, gathered them and provided them with words from Sacred Scripture and from the discipline of the Rule in good conversations. Yet some of them, regarding me in a bad light, attacked me in secret with their words, saying that they could not bear the harshness of the discipline of the rule to which I wanted to bind them. But God gave me consolation in other good and wise sisters who had assisted me in all my sufferings, the same as he had done for Susanna [the biblical personage] whom God liberated from the false witnesses. [Hildegard continues:] Despite all the toil of the tribulations of this sort that weakened me, nonetheless I was able to finish, by the grace of God, *The Book of the Merits of Life* that was divinely revealed to me.

Beset by difficulties of a material nature as well as by

those caused by the conduct of the religious whose abbess she was, Hildegard still pursued no less at Rupertsberg the task that was hers: the writing of the second of her works, *The Book of the Merits of Life.*

Moreover, this was not her sole activity, since it is likely that her musical compositions kept her busy throughout her life. As for her two books that deal with medicine and natural sciences, there is nothing in the biographical accounts indicating the time when she wrote them. One cannot call to mind the life of the nuns and of Hildegard herself without taking into account the visitors who from then onward crowded around Bingen. The local population had welcomed her "with great exultation and divine praises," yet it was not just from the surrounding region that visitors streamed. As Bernard Gorceix writes, citing Hildegard's biography: "One would have said that, after the Synod of Trier, the Catholic world was in movement . . . pilgrims arrived on horseback and on foot even from distant regions."

One of these visitors especially attracted the attention of the authors of the saint's biography—even though they do not state his name (book two, chapter three):

The Lord helped [the abbess] not just in the pain of sickness or the assault of demons, but also when she had to bear the attacks of humans; God turned the hearts of her adversaries for the better, as she herself relates with regard to the conversion of a philosopher, who at first was hostile not only to her

but also to God himself; and in whom thereafter was achieved
the change directed by the hand of the Most High. . . .

This philosopher, whose name is not given, may have
been a scholar; in any case, he was an unbeliever, skeptical
about this nun whose lights were highly praised.

This philosopher, abounding in riches, after long doubting
what I had seen, finally came to us and provided our dwelling
with structures, furnishings, and other badly needed things;
this made our soul rejoice, for God had not let these things be
forgotten. After a detailed but wise inquiry, he asked what
were and where were the writings of this vision, and came to
believe fully in the divine inspiration. He at first had expressed
to us his contempt in words full of malice. Once God had
done much for the justice in his heart, he turned toward us
with the greatest blessings: just as God drowned Pharaoh in
the Red Sea, the one who wanted to seize the children of
Israel. By the marvel of this change, many people believed
from then on, and God sent down his blessing on us through
that wise man . . . so much so that we all called him our father.
And he, who at first was designated as a prince by his name,
asked to be buried among us, and that is what was done.

In contrast to this unbeliever who finally became convinced, many people came to the inspired abbess in search
of peace of heart or of physical healing. Hildegard's biographers list the numerous occurrences which then seemed

miraculous in everyone's eyes; these are less convincing, of course, for today's reader than is the enormous correspondence through which she dispensed her advice, indeed her warnings, to all sorts of authorities, spiritual as well as temporal. In order to understand the reason and the range of the influence of this little nun from the banks of the Rhine on the tumultuous world surrounding her, it is good to do as the philosopher whom she mentions: turn to the first work that she wrote, the work that received pontifical approval as well as that of Saint Bernard, the *Scivias*.

CHAPTER III

THE SCIVIAS

IT IS EVIDENTLY IMPOSSIBLE to know which passage from the *Scivias* was read by the pope before the Synod of Trier. We at least know that it was something from the early chapters of the book, those which had been written by 1147, since the entire book was not finished until 1151. The *Scivias* contains three books: the first describes six visions of Hildegard, followed by her commentary on them; the second, seven visions; and the third, thirteen. The last of the visions of the third book ends with a kind of theater piece, or rather an opera, in which the virtues are personified and sustain attacks by the demon; Hildegard would return to this in a full musical work called *Ordo virtutum (Order of Virtues)*.

Since the specific passage read by the pope will always remain unknown to us, we can choose from the first book of *Scivias* the third vision, very characteristic of the tone that the author maintains thereafter throughout her work.

I saw an immense round sphere filled with shadow, in the shape of an egg, not so large at the top, wider in the middle, and narrower at the bottom; in its outer part it had a circle of sparkling light and under it a dark covering. And in this circle of flames there was a blazing globe, so large that the whole sphere was illumined by it. Above it there were, arranged in order, three stars that kept the globe itself in its fiery activity, lest it fall little by little. This globe raised itself higher and gave more light, so that it could cast its flaming rays further. And then sometimes it lowered itself, and the cold was more intense since it had withdrawn its flame.

From this web of flames that surrounded the sphere, the wind blew with its swirls, and from the dark covering that surrounded the web of flames, another wind with its swirls resounded and spread in every direction over the sphere. In this same covering there was a dark fire that inspired such great horror that I could not look at it, and that, full of troubles and storms, and filled with sharp stones, small and large, this covering shook with all its power. While it made its crackling heard, the luminous circle and the winds and the air were stirring, so that the lightning flashes warned of the rumbling, because this fire felt within itself the commotion that the tumult caused, yet above the same covering the sky was very clear and had no cloud above.

And in the sky I discerned a globe of burning fire, of a certain greatness, and above it two stars that evidently held the globe back so that it would not stray from the aim of its course. And in the same sky, many other luminous spheres were situated all over, among which was the same globe, pouring out a bit, at times shed its light; and turning to the first fire of the blazing globe to restore its flame, it sent it again toward the same spheres.

Then from the sky itself a gust of wind with its swirls burst out and spread over the whole heavenly sphere. Under the sky itself, I saw the humid air that held a cloud below; this cloud, spreading to all sides, extended this humidity over the whole sphere. When this humidity accumulated, a sudden rain fell with much noise. And after it was gently poured out, a fine rain fell with a very light murmur. Then a wind with its swirls burst out to spread over the whole sphere. In the midst of all these elements was a sandy globe of immense expanse, which the same elements surrounded in such a way that it could not disappear, neither in one direction nor in another. And while the same elements with their different gusts struggled together, they forced that sandy globe to move a little by its power. And I saw between Aquilo and Orient (the North and the East) something like a great mountain that cast many shadows toward Aquilo, and toward Orient much light. . . .

And I heard again a voice from heaven saying to me: "God, who has made all things by his will, has created them for the knowledge and honor of his name, not only to show in them visible and temporal things, but also to manifest in them invisible and eternal things. This is shown by the vision that you are contemplating."

Hildegard proceeds to explain this vision. For her, the object described at the beginning—the round and shaded sphere—is a sign of God. She comments, "In early times, humans were rough and simple in their customs; then, in the Old and the New Law, having become more instructed, they mutually troubled and afflicted each other. Yet at the end of ages, they will have to suffer many misfortunes in their hardening. . . ."

She states that the shaded covering that surrounds the flame stands for those who are outside the faith.

In this flame, the globe—of a sparkling fire, of grandeur so great that it brightens the whole sphere—shows by the splendor of its clarity what is within God the Father: his only ineffable Son, the sun of justice burning with ardent charity and possessing such great glory that every creature is illumined by its clarity and its light. And the globe of fire sometimes turns downwards . . . to signify that the same only Son of God, born of a Virgin and mercifully lowered toward the poverty of humans, bore all corporal infirmities and left the world in order to return to his father. . . . This means: the children of the Church having received the Son of God in the interior knowledge of their heart, the holiness of his body was lifted up by the power of his divinity and, in a mystical miracle, the night of the secret mystery abducted him to hide him from mortal eyes, for the elements are at his service.

She then explains that one of the gusts of wind is a sign of God who fills the universe with his omnipotence, and that the other impetuous wind that rages with its swirls comes from Satan's anger, out of which "the notorious wickedness issues . . . that spreads on every direction over the sphere, for in the world useful or useless rumors are mingled in various ways among the nations." She means that murder is mixed with avarice, drunkenness, and the cruelest evil deeds.

"Then," she adds,

> above this covering, the sky is very pure and without veil, since under the pitfalls of the old deceiver luminous faith shines. . . . It does not come on its own, but is based on Christ. And in this sky, you see a globe of burning fire, very large in size, which truly designates the Church, united in the faith, as that whiteness of innocent clarity shows it, forming an aura of glory for it; and above it, two stars set apart . . . show that two Testaments, of the old and of the new authority, lead the Church. . . .
>
> Under the same sky, you see the humid air and, underneath, a white cloud that spreading in every direction, scatters the humidity over the whole sphere. [This is the image of baptism] uncovering to the whole universe the source of salvation for believers. . . . From it, a wind with its swirls issued and spread over the whole sphere so that, from the spread of baptism that brought salvation to believers, the true fame propagating with words—of learned discourse—penetrated the whole world . . . among the nations that abandoned faithlessness in order to embrace the Catholic faith.

Finally, the sandy globe designates man and the world created for his use. Hildegard's commentary becomes a prayer here:

> O God, you who have wondrously made all things, you have

crowned man with the golden crown of understanding; and you have vested him with the superb garment of visible beauty; in setting him as a prince, above your perfect works, which you have arranged with justice and kindness among your creatures. For you have endowed man with dignities greater and more admirable than those you granted to other creatures.

A moment of contemplation, during which Hildegard expresses a sentiment that is found elsewhere in her work: wonder before the beauty of creation, a familiar sentiment in her time, the same one that is admirably felt and expressed in the work of a Hugh of Saint Victor: "God has willed not only that the world might be, but that it might also be beautiful and magnificent."

Another aspect then comes into view, when the visionary explains what the great mountain signifies that lies between Aquilo, the place of darkness, and Orient, the place of light. The fall of man is evoked here, which occurred

"through the abominable lie of the evil spirit who causes the multiple miseries of damnation for reprobates. [The mountain evokes] those kinds of people who stubbornly test me [God] by their perverse skill, scrutinizing the creature made for their service and asking it to show them according to their wish what they want to know: Can they, by their questing skill, prolong or shorten the time of life that has been set by the Creator? This they surely cannot do, neither for a day nor for an hour. Or can they deflect predestination by God? Not at all, but I [God] allow that creatures sometimes show you your passions and their distinctive signs, since they fear me as their God. . . . O foolish ones, when you try to forget me, and wish not to return to me and adore me, and when you look to creatures to know what they predict for you or what they tell you, you then renounce me stubbornly and you honor weak creatures in preference to your Creator."

This is aimed against all efforts at divination. In continuation:

"Yet sometimes the stars, with my permission, show themselves to humans with signs as my Son tells in the Gospel when he says: 'There will be signs in the sun, in the moon and in the stars.' This means: by the brightness of those stars, humans will be illumined; and the times of times will be shown by their evolution. Thus, in the end times, some lamentable and perilous periods will be manifest in them by my permission, so that the rays of the sun, the splendor of the moon and the brightness of the stars will sometimes disappear in order to stir the hearts of human beings."

The visionary then takes the example of the star that guided the Magi in order to show that, while it is false that a person has a "particular star" for arranging his or her life, as stupid people and those who abuse themselves try to believe, nonetheless this star has shined "because my [God's] only Son was born through a sinless Virgin giving birth. But this star gave no help to my Son other than by announcing faithfully to the people his incarnation. for all stars and creatures who fear him accomplish only my will. They have no other meaning of any kind in any creature at all."

Thus she attacks astrology and every sort of divination, everything that misleads human piety and understanding away from the divine mystery:

"I do not want you to scrutinize the stars, or fire, or fowl, or any other creature at all, on future matters."

And, pursuing these errors and satanic sorcery, the visionary again lets God address humans:

"O human, I have bought you with the blood of my Son, not with malice and iniquity, but with the greatest justice. And yet you abandon me, the true God, and you follow the one who is the liar. I am justice and truth, and this is why I call you in faith, I exhort you in love, and I lead you in penance, so that, even though bloodied by the wounds of sin, you might still rise from the depths of your fall."

Following the commentary on the vision, she adds this appeal that was dictated to her by the splendor that she perceived:

"O foolish humans, why do you as creatures worry about the times of your lives? None of you can know the time of your life, nor avoid or pass around what has been set by me. For, O human, when your salvation, both in temporal things or in spiritual ones, is accomplished, you will exchange the present age in order to pass into the one that has no end. For, since a human possesses so great a power that he can love me more ardently than other creatures . . . I will not separate his spirit from his body until he has been able to bring to their ripeness its savory fruits that have a sweet fragrance. But the one whom I consider to be so weak that he cannot bear my yoke among the temptations of the evil seducer and in the burdensome slavery of his body, him I withdraw from this age before he begins to wither in the time of the withering of his soul; for I know all. I wish to give to the human race all justice to safeguard it, so that no one can find an excuse when I call and exhort human beings to accomplish the works of justice, when I instill in them the fear of the Judgment of death, as if they were about to die soon, even though they might have still a long time to live. . . .

In the following vision, the fourth of the *Scivias,* this questioning on the destiny of man continues, still by way of images and by following therein the developmental stages of human life.

I saw an immense and serene splendor, shining as from many eyes, with its four corners turned to the four parts of the world, which, by indicating the secret of the supreme Creator, was manifested to me in a great mystery; and in this serene splendor, another splendor like the dawn, having in itself a brightness of a crimson glow, appeared. . . . And I saw something like the form of a woman having in its breast something of the perfect form of a man, and then by a secret disposition of the supreme Creator, this same form manifested the movement of life; and a blazing sphere, having no feature of a human body, possessed the heart of this form, touched its brain and spread into all its members; and then this form of man, vivified in this manner, rising from the woman's bosom, had movements conforming to those of humans on this sphere and changed its color in accord with their colors.

The time of tribulations, then, will come for this human form whom the fall has exposed to all its dangers:

I, a stranger, where am I? In the shadow of death? What is the path that I follow—the way of error—and what consolation can I enjoy, that of pilgrims; indeed, I should have had a stone tabernacle, more resplendent than the sun and the stars, since the setting sun and the fading stars should not shine on it, but it should be filled with angelic glory, because topaz should serve as its foundation and all gems should form its structure; its steps should be of pure glass and its courtyard draped in gold, for I should be the companion of angels, since I am the living breath that God instilled into dry matter; this is why I should know God and love him. But when my tabernacle [the human body, tabernacle of the Holy Spirit] comprehended that it could with its eyes look in every direction [a sign of the freedom granted to a human, of his possibility for choice, of his desire to choose for himself what is its good or its evil], it turned toward Aquilo [the place of cold and distress].

All of the creatures' woes then follow:

Some sought to cover me with shame; they made me eat the food of swine and, sending me into a desert place, they also gave me bitter herbs soaked in honey to eat. Then, stretching me on a press, they afflicted me with many torments and, stripping me of my garments to wound me in many places, they left me as the prey of beasts; serpents and venomous scorpions, asps and others of that kind seized me and riddled me with their venom.

The victim of all torments, she cries out:

Where are you, Zion, O my Mother. Woe is me because I have fled, alas, far from you! . . . But when I shed my tears on you, O my Mother, with my groaning, wretched Babylon makes the roaring of its water resound so much that you cannot be attentive to my voice. That is why I must search for the narrow paths over which I can flee from my dreadful companions and my hateful captivity. After speaking so, I went along a narrow path where, bitterly sobbing, I hid in a small cave on the northern side, because I had lost my Mother. Then a pleasant odor arose, as if coming from the sweet breath of my Mother, enchanting me with its perfume. . . . And I was so carried away with joy that the mountain cavern where I had taken refuge rang with my cries of gladness. . . . I wanted to scale a height where my enemies could not discover me, but they placed a troubled sea in my way that made it impossible for me to cross. A bridge was there that was so narrow and small that I could no longer go over it. Yet within this sea stood mountains whose peaks were so high that I felt it impossible to reach them.

Fallen again into her terror, the creature once again calls upon the power on high.

I then heard my Mother's voice saying to me: "Run, daughter, because wings have been given to you so that you might fly, by the mighty giver whom nothing can resist; fly, then, above these annoyances, with all the speed of your wings." Again I arrived before a tabernacle built on indestructible bases and, entering it, I performed the works of light after having carried on the works of darkness. And in this tabernacle, on the north, I set an unpolished iron column on which I hung several wings here and there that shook like fans; finding manna there, I ate it. But on the east I built a fort of squared stones and, lighting a fire there, I drank some sweet wine mixed with myrrh. On the south, I built also a tower on which I hung shields colored red, and on the windows I set ivory trumpets. In the middle of this tower I poured honey, from which I made a precious perfume with other spices, so that its powerful fragrance spread throughout the tabernacle. On the west, I built nothing, since that part was turned toward the age.

Again exposed to all the assaults of hate and deceit, the creature implores God's help:

And I heard a voice again saying to me: "The blessed and ineffable Trinity was manifested to this world when the Father sent into the world his only Son, conceived by the Holy Spirit and born of the Virgin, so that humans born in many different conditions, held by the bonds of sin, might be led by Christ in the way of Truth."

The necessary clarifications were given little by little, so that humans might be saved.

The next part bears an elucidation of the vision stated first:

This female form which you see, carrying in its womb a perfect human form, means that after a woman has received human seed, the child is formed with the integrity of its members in the hidden cell of its mother's womb. By a secret disposition of the divine Creator, the same form shows the movement of life because, in virtue of an order and of the mysterious will of God, the child has received the spirit in the maternal womb, at the moment established and willed by God; it shows by its body's movements that it lives, just as the earth opens up and lets bloom the flowers of its fruit when the dew has descended upon it. In this manner, it is like a sphere of flames, having no feature of the human body, possessing the heart of this form because the soul blazing in the hearth of sovereign knowledge distinguished different things in the circle of its understanding. And this sphere has no feature of the human body because it is neither corporal nor ephemeral as is the human body, and because it gives power and life. And being the foundation of the body, it rules it entirely. . . . Moreover, this human form thus vivified in its mother's womb possesses when it comes out the movements that the flaming sphere within it impresses on it. And, following its movements, it also changes its color because, after a human has received in the womb of his mother the breath of life, and is born, and has shown the movements of his acts, according to the works that the soul accomplishes with the body, the merits come to him from these very works, for he is robed with the splendor of good works and is sheltered from the darkness of the wicked.

This same flaming sphere shows its vigor, following corporal energies, in such a way that in a human's childhood it displays its simplicity, in the youth of power, and in the fullness of age . . . it manifests the power of its virtues by its wisdom. . . . But a human has inside three paths [three ways or manners of being]. What are they? The soul, the body, and the senses, and it is through them that life is conducted. How? The soul vivifies the body and contains thought, and the body draws the soul and manifests thought, while the senses touch the soul and please the body. For the soul gives life to the body, as fire makes light penetrate into darkness, by means of two main powers that it possesses: intellect and will, which are as its two arms. [Since she rejects simplistic interpretations, Hildegard promptly adds:] It is not that the soul has two arms for moving itself, but because it manifests itself by these two forces as does the sun by its splendor. [Intellect and will are the two means that a human has for manifesting himself.]

Farther on, after describing the possibilities of the human being, Hildegard expresses once again through her vision the tendencies of a human:

The soul in the body is like sap in a tree, and its faculties are like the branches of a tree. How so? Intellect is in the soul like the greenness of the branches and leaves, the will like flowers, the spirit like the first fruit that springs from it, reason like the perfect fruit that becomes ripe, the senses like the extension of its grandeur. It is in this manner that the human body is strengthened and supported by the soul. This is why, O human, you must understand what you are because of your soul, you who renounce your understanding and who want to be compared to animals.

After the stages of human destiny, the times of the Revelation develops the fifth vision, with the image of the Church succeeding that of the Synagogue.

I saw something like a woman's image, white from the head down to the navel, black from the navel down to the feet, and the feet the color of blood. Around her feet she had a shining and pure cloud. She lacked eyes and, holding her hands over her armpits, stayed near the altar that is before the eyes of God; but she did not touch it. And in her heart was Abraham; and in her bosom, Moses; and in her belly the other prophets, each one showing his sign and admiring the beauty of the new bride. She appeared as large as the immense tower of that city, having on her head something like a halo similar to the dawn. And I heard again a voice from heaven saying to me: "God imposed on the ancient people the austerity of the Law by establishing circumcision for Abraham. He then changed it into a grace of mildness, by giving his Son to those who believe in the truth of the Gospel. And he comforted with the oil of mercy those who had been wounded by the yoke of the Law. This is why you see something like a woman's image, white from head to navel: this is the Synagogue, mother of the incarnation of the Son of God and who from the beginning of the birth of her children, up till the fullness of their powers, foresees in the shadows the secrets of God, but does not uncover them fully. For she is not the resplendent dawn that appears openly, but the one who looks from afar with astonishment and admiration. . . . The Synagogue admires the new bride, the Church, who is not seen adorned with the same virtues as she is, but surrounded with angelic escorts, so that the demon can neither ruin her nor turn her back; whereas the Synagogue, abandoned by God, lies in vice. . . . Her feet are all bloody, and around her feet a gleaming cloud shines because, at her consummation, she put to death Christ, the Prophet of prophets; she herself, fallen, then collapsed. However, in this consummation, the pure and shining light of faith arose in the spirit of believers because, at the moment of the Synagogue's fall, the Church arose, when the apostolic teaching, after the death of the Son of God, spread throughout the earth."

By contrast with the Synagogue, the Church

appears so majestic that it is comparable to the high tower of a city, because, accepting the beauty of the divine precepts, she armed and fortified the noble city of the elect. She has on her head a halo resembling the dawn, because the Church in her birth manifested the miracle of the Son of God, as well as the radiant virtues and the mysteries that flow from it. . . . Now, just as man, by the death of the only Son of God, in a new age, was snatched from the perdition of death, so also the Synagogue, before the Last Day, drawn by the divine clemency, will abandon unbelief and will truly attain the knowledge of God. . . . Thus, the Synagogue goes ahead in the shadow of the figure, and the Church follows in the light of truth.

This grand image of the opposition between the Synagogue with veiled eyes and the Church contemplating the divine mystery was familiar in Hildegard's age. Suffice it to recall the magnificent southern portal of the cathedral of Strasbourg, where this double vision is found expressed in stone; or again, a little later, this same double image on the portal of the cathedral of Bamberg, Church and Synagogue resplendent in like beauty.

These extracts from the first book of the *Scivias* give an idea of the whole of Hildegard's work. These are visions of powerful originality, both rich and precise, which in her eyes unfold with a great wealth of details and colors that are very typical of an era of great creativity. They are violent visions, where it seems that all descriptions are pushed to excess. While the themes are well-known, being those of the Incarnation, of the Redemption, of Creation itself, they are developed here with a power that renews them, outside of conventional formulations, exempt from any weakness or dullness; inflamed pages, streams of images that provoke the questions "How so?" and "What is this?"—and which extend the interpretations given by the seer for detailing their meaning and scope.

Broad visions sometimes conceal sumptuous comparisons, in which gems and topaz, iron pillars and ivory trumpets, make up a kind of fairyland, and are sometimes stamped with a simplicity very close to nature: "the soul in the body like sap in a tree and its faculties like branches." Even traditional and familiar images of the age such as that of the Synagogue and the Church find in them a new sumptuousness: "white from the head down to the navel, black down to the feet and with the feet the color of blood."

Nothing less than an earnest awareness of biblical images was needed, to which the accents of the prophets were familiar, in order to perceive this inflamed expression of truths fundamental to Christians. One can understand how Saint Bernard recognized in this "a shining light." Hildegard renews for her times, with an unexpected violence, the expression of the mysteries that the Bible teaches and that the Church transmits. And her whole work thus casts a new gaze, ardent and enchanting in its simplicity, on the content of faith.

CHAPTER IV

LIFE IN THE MONASTERY OF BINGEN

AT THE TIME THAT HILDEGARD was finishing the *Scivias*, while establishing her foundation in Bingen, which would remain attached to her name, an incident occurred, bearing a human mark—one might even say, sentimental—in the unfolding of this uncommon life.

We have mentioned the presence, on some miniatures that represent the visionary, of a young nun standing behind her, who is generally identified as Richardis, her secretary; like Volmar, the monk, she is inseparable from the redaction of the *Scivias*. Richardis was the daughter of the marchioness of Stade, who helped Hildegard greatly in the foundation of her monastery at Bingen. Her brother, Hartwig, was archbishop of Bremen. It is probable that Richardis performed the role of the abbess's secretary, and that she assisted her in the various offices of the convent. It is in this context that she must have had a part, albeit secondary, in the redaction of the *Scivias*.

Now, in 1151, Richardis herself was elected abbess of a monastery in Saxony, Bassum, in the diocese of Bremen. Upon learning about it, Hildegard hastened to write to her mother: "Do not go and distract my soul and make bitter tears fall from my eyes and fill my heart with cruel wounds with regard to my dearest daughters, Richardis and Adelaide [Richardis's sister]." It seems that she used all her power to prevent these two young religious from leaving. Yet clearly the archbishop of Bremen wanted this transfer, and in this case he had the support and approval of that other prelate who until then had helped Hildegard greatly, at the time of her establishment in Bingen—Archbishop Henry of Mainz. The abbess thus saw Richardis go away, and this departure was very painful for her. She tried to approach her brother Hartwig to have her returned to Rupertsberg, but was rebuffed; she then went so far as to write to the pope, Eugene III. We possess neither her letter nor the pontiff's reply, but he could have only sent it on to local authorities. However, there is a letter from Hildegard to Richardis that has been preserved for us: "I loved the nobility of your comportment, the wisdom and the purity of your soul and of your whole being." An affinity of this sort could only have made the separation wrenching.

The next year, at the end of 1152, Archbishop Hartwig of Bremen wrote to Hildegard to inform her about his sister's sudden death. He also told her that Richardis had shed many tears over her first cloister and had been making plans to visit Hildegard when death overtook her:

I am informing you that our sister, mine but even more yours, mine by the flesh, yours by the soul, has gone the way of all flesh. . . . She piously made a holy confession, and was anointed with holy oil after her confession, while conducting herself fully as a Christian, she who had wept over your cloister with many heartfelt tears. She then commended herself to the Lord, with his Mother and Saint John. Marked with the sign of the cross, confessing the Trinity and unity of God in perfect faith, in hope and in charity, we are certain, she died on the fourth day of the calends of November [October 28]. I ask you, then, if I am worthy of it, as much as I can, that you keep your love for her as much as she loved you. If it seems to you that she committed some fault in anything, do not impute it to her but rather to me, taking into account her tears which she shed after leaving your cloister, as many witnesses can attest. Had her death not prevented her, as soon as she would have received permission, she would have gone to see you. Since her death prevented this, I will come to pay you a visit, God willing. . . .

In her response, Hildegard first renders homage to Richardis's brother, wishing for him that God keep his eyes on him and guide him toward the fulfillment of his holy will. She continues:

For me, poor little figure that I am, I have seen in you a light of salvation. Fulfill for now the precepts of God who gives you his grace, and fulfill what the Holy Spirit teaches you. . . . May your eye see God, your mind understand his justice, and your heart burn with God's love so that your soul might not weaken, but that it might use extreme zeal in building the tower of the heavenly Jerusalem, and that God give you a helper, namely the sweet Mother of mercy. Be a bright star shining in the darkness of the nights of depraved humans, and be a speedy stag running to the fountain of living water.

After vigorously calling to mind the needs of the Church in that age, Hildegard continues in stirring phrases:

For now, listen: thus it was done with my daughter Richardis. I call her my daughter, for in my soul there was complete charity toward her, since the living Light, in a very powerful vision, taught me to love her as myself. Listen: God kept her in a zeal so great that the attraction of the world could not hold her, but it assailed her even though she appeared in the symphony of this world as a flower in her beauty and her splendor. Yet at the time that she was still living in her body, I heard this about her in a true vision: "O virginity, keep yourself in the royal chamber." She, indeed, was in the most holy order of virgins and was in their company, of which the daughters of Zion rejoice. . . . This is why God did not want to give his beloved to the enemy lover, namely to the world. For now, dear one, sitting in Christ's place, fulfill the wish of your sister as the need for obedience requires; just as she was always concerned over you, so have concern for her soul and do good works after the zeal that was hers. . . . " [Letter ten and its response.]

One is struck by the serenity that flows from this missive; Hartwig's letter, however, was marked by emotion above all: The abbess had evidently mastered her own disappointment and carried out the sacrifice required.

This sad episode happened probably around 1151, when Hildegard finished the *Scivias.* The writer of her *Life,* with much less detail than we would have wished, sheds some light on the years that followed in the Bingen convent. He marvels at seeing that a stream of good works flowed from her, as if she had watered them from the river of paradise, and that "not only from the whole town, but also from all of Tripartite Gaul and from Germany" people streamed toward the abbess; from everywhere people of both sexes came seeking her counsel and exhortation. Many also came to see her in order to have corporal afflictions healed. Some, thanks to her blessing, were relieved of their sufferings. In a prophetic spirit, she knew people's thoughts and intentions, and would turn away those approaching her in a perverse or frivolous spirit, as if to test her. Since they could not resist the spirit that spoke, they were obliged, chastened and purified, to abandon their twisted plan. Jews who, convinced of their law, came to see her to ask her questions, she would exhort to the faith of Christ in words of pious admonitions. To everyone, according to the Apostle's advice, she would speak sweetly and affectionately as seemed fitting to her for each one.

The *Life* of Hildegard reports on some of the miracles that are attributed to her. These are mostly healings, from illnesses that are at times only vaguely described. She relieved one of her relatives of a fever that no one had been able to treat. Further, in an unnamed monastery a servant named Bertha had a tumor on the neck that prevented her from swallowing any food or drink, not even her saliva; a sign of the cross traced on the painful swelling was enough to free her from it. Sometimes Hildegard limited herself to sending some holy water to those who sought her help, and their pains would ease. This was the case with a mother who requested healing for her daughter; and the holy water sent by the abbess also took care of a young man who had fallen into a state of extreme weakness. Some of the healings show how widely Hildegard's fame had reached. Thus, a certain Sibyl wrote to her from the city of Lausanne beyond the Alps in order to be freed from a "flow of blood"—which indeed happened after an answer from Hildegard. Again, a young man of Andernach, who had supplicated the Lord while invoking Hildegard's intercession, saw her appear and place her hand on his head and say, "Let this illness go away from you, and be healed." As soon as the vision disappeared, the sick man got up from his bed.

Another miracle occurred in touching circumstances, during a journey that Hildegard was making along the Rhine in order to go to one of the towns where she had been called to preach. On the boat, a woman showed her her little boy who was blind. "Hildegard," the text reads, "remembering the One who said, 'Go to the pool of Siloam and wash yourself,' took some water from the river in her left hand and blessed the boy with her right hand while pouring the water over his eyes. Immediately, as granted by divine grace, he recovered his sight." A valuable indication is given to us in this passage about Hildegard's journeys; most of them had to be done, as we shall see, by river; besides, it was the most common mode of transportation in that age.

It was at Bingen, doubtless between 1158 and 1163, that the abbess wrote her second work, entitled *The Book of the Merits of Life*. It contains six visions, grouped into a single book, whereas the *Scivias* contained three books with as many themes. The first work had as its subject the Creator and the creature; as Bernard Gorceix analyzes it in his admirable introduction to Hildegard's work, "the second the Messiah and the Church, the third the history of salvation." He continues: "In the second text, *The Book of the Merits of Life,* the structure is monolithic: in the course of six successive visions, a human figure looks in the direction of the east, the west, the north and then the south, then the entire universe in a fifth stage. In six only, the human figure enters into movement with the four zones of the Earth. This human figure is no one else but God." In short, this *Book of the Merits* deals with salvation's history, with the comparison of virtues and vices and the triumph of divinity.

Finally, it was in 1163 that Hildegard undertook her third work, *The Book of Divine Works*—better-known since Bernard Gorceix translated it and it was published in French in 1982.

In 1165, Hildegard founded a new monastery. Undoubtedly the number of religious was beginning to exceed the capacity of the accommodations of the Bingen convent. Without changing region, on the other side of the Rhine, above Rüdesheim, the third foundation, that of Eibingen, was opened. In its very name it preserves that of Saint Hildegard, and it represents today the only foundation in existence where the abbess had lived, since the other two were completely destroyed by the Swedish invasion in the seventeenth century. It is there, as we have said, that the tomb of Hildegard is located, in the chapel rebuilt in the sixteenth century and remodeled in our day. Mosaics reproduce some of her visions.

Certain episodes in Hildegard's life are known to us through her correspondence, which gives us a more personal echo of it than the biographical narrative. This is the case with the healing of Sigewise, a young woman of Cologne who seems to have displayed a case of demonic possession. Letters were exchanged on the matter between Hildegard and the monks of the abbey of Brauweiler, who had tried unsuccessfully to liberate this woman. Their correspondence attests the trust that they had in the nun.

The abbot of Brauweiler addresses her in terms that give evidence of her reputation:

> Although, beloved lady, your face is unknown to us, the fame of your virtues makes you greatly celebrated and, although

absent in body, nonetheless in spirit we are assiduously present to you. . . . Among us, we have heard it told about what
has been done through you by the Lord, who has accomplished great things through you, he who is mighty and whose
name is holy.

Thus it is on the basis of this fame of Hildegard that he
addresses her, imploring her advice on a case that he cannot resolve:

A certain noblewoman, obsessed by an evil spirit for several
years, was brought to us by friendly hands so that she might
be delivered from the enemy menacing her, by the help of Saint
Nicholas under whose patronage we are placed. However, the
cleverness and wickedness of this very cunning and detestable
enemy have led so many people by the thousands into error
and doubt that we fear greatly that he might become a great
danger for the holy Church. Indeed, all of us with many other
people have been working to liberate this woman in different
ways for three months, and, we cannot say without grief,
because of our sins we have achieved nothing; thus all our
hope is in you after God. Indeed, this demon, one day when
conjured up, ended by making known to us that this obsessed
woman could not be liberated except by the power of your
contemplation and the grandeur of divine revelation. . . . We
therefore ask your holiness to tell us kindly by letter what God
has been able to inspire in you or reveal to you through visions
on this matter.

Hildegard's answer first contains advice on a line of action to pursue:

Since she has been afflicted by a long and serious illness with God's permission, I can very rightly answer something of your question; I say this not by myself, but by him who is: there are different kinds of evil spirits. The demon about whom you speak has artifices that are similar to vices in human customs. Thus he willingly dwells among humans; he also laughs and cares little for the cross of God, for the saints, etc.; anything that belongs to the service of God he does not fear much. He does not love him but pretends to flee him, just as a foolish and careless man scorns the words and the threats that wise people address to him. This one is more difficult to get rid of than any other demon. He cannot be driven out without fasts, mortifications, prayers, alms, and by God's own order. Listen, then, to the answer not of a human, but of him who lives. Choose seven good witnesses whose merits of life recommend them, who are priests, in the name and in the order of Abel, Noah, Abraham, Melchisedech, Jacob, and Aaron, who will offer a sacrifice to the living God, and the seventh in the name of Christ who offered himself on the cross to God the Father. Through fasts, flagellations, prayers, alms, and celebration of Masses with humble intention and in priestly garments, let them be vested with their stoles toward the patient and let them surround her, each one holding in his hand a staff, as a figure of the staff with which Moses in Egypt struck the Red Sea and the rock according to God's precept, so that, just as

God showed miracles there through the staff, so also may this wicked enemy be rejected by the staffs and God be glorified by this. . . . These priests will be seven, as a figure of the seven gifts of the Holy Spirit, so that the Spirit of God, who in the beginning was borne above the waters and who inspired the breath of life in man's face, might turn away the unclean spirit of the weary human. . . .

Some time later, the monks of the abbey of Brauweiler returned to the task. The spirit, conjured according to Hildegard's instructions, had at first indeed left in peace the person in question, but once again it had taken possession of her. Thus they now asked the abbess's permission to bring to her this female victim of the evil spirit, convinced that she would be cured only in Hildegard's presence. At that time Hildegard was gravely ill, but the young noblewoman (this is how she is always designated), obsessed by the demon, was nonetheless brought to the monastery. She was full of scorn for the old abbess, whom she mocked by calling her Scrumpilgard ("Wrinklegard"), a derisive pun on her name.

Finally, at the urging of the monks of Brauweiler, who for several years tried without success to conjure the demon assailing this woman, Hildegard decided to receive her. She said,

We have been disturbed at the arrival of this woman, how we could see her and listen to her, she by whom many people were tormented over a long period. Yet God kindly willed to send his dew of his sweetness upon us and we have been able to have her come in and lodge her in the house of sisters without the help of men. Since then we have not ceased to concern ourselves with her, despite the horror or the confusion lest the demon intervene because of our sins, nor despite the scornful and derisive words by which she wanted to call us, nor for her very detestable behavior. And I saw that there were three stages of suffering in this woman: first, when she was led from her room to the place of the "saints" [in the sanctuary], then when the common people gave alms for her, and, third, when by the prayers of the Holy Spirit she was obliged to go away [the evil spirit goes away] by the grace of God.

The whole convent was in prayer, extending into fasts, recital of prayers, and alms since the day of the Purification of Our Lady (February 2), up till Easter Saturday.

Many people became more courageous in the faith, many were led to become more fervent and to confess their sins. . . . On Holy Saturday, at the point when the baptismal water is consecrated, under the breath of the priest, which he cast over the font with the words that the Holy Spirit had taught to the doctors of the Church and to human reason . . . the woman who was present there, seized by great terror, began to tremble so much that with her feet she pounded the floor and emitted several breaths of the horrible spirit who had oppressed her. Soon, in a true vision, I saw and understood that the power of the Most High, that had covered the baptismal fonts and was covering them again, said to the diabolic troop by which this woman was obsessed: "Go away, Satan, from the tabernacle of the body of this woman, and leave room in her for the Holy Spirit." Then the unclean spirit went out of that woman as in horrible vomitings, and she was liberated. From then on she remained healthy in her senses of spirit and body, as she still lives in the present time. When this became known by the people, everyone with canticles of praise and many with all sorts of prayers were saying, "Glory to you, Lord," recalling the example of Job over whom Satan could not have complete power. . . . God did not permit that this woman, who had been freed from the evil spirit, should have her soul stricken in her good faith; the enemy was confounded in her, for he could not turn her away from the justice of God.

So reads the text of the *Life* of Hildegard, adding that she would tell the story "sweetly, gently, in all humility, and attributing nothing of it to herself."

Parallel to this exorcism story, which to some people may seem improbable, Hildegard's correspondence offers numerous cases in which the visionary speaks of remedies of simple common sense and puts her correspondents on guard against all exaggeration, excessive mortification, etc. This was the case in regard to Hazzecha, whose troubles showed a simple instability of character, although Hildegard was asked on several occasions to bring some remedy into play. This Hazzecha was the abbess of an important monastery, that of Krauftal. Hildegard, as we shall see, stopped there during her second journey which she made around the year 1160 heading to Cologne. It is after her stay in the monastery that Hazzecha approached her. She was visibly distressed: she shared with the visionary the anxiety in which she found herself, and sought to gain from her some light that she was lacking.

She writes,

After I had gained, with God's help, the aid of your longed-for presence and your affability, I was relieved of the fear in my spirit and of the first trial undergone. And since your word, I have no doubt, proceeds not from a human spirit but rather from the true light that has enlightened you more than other people, I have waited at your advice to do up till the present what you suggested to me. I wish to know, dearest lady and sister, you whom I have so longed to see for the first time—I wish to do so no less at present, and since I cannot do so in the body, I always attach myself to you through my heart—and since it is certain that charity is in you and that you are in charity, I ask you by this charity not to delay in writing to me what this living Light has manifested to you in spirit about me, and which may be worthy to be corrected or adopted.

Hildegard's answer is brief and unambiguous.

He who sees all says: "You have eyes for seeing and for looking all around. Wherever you see dirt, wash it away and make green whatever is dry, yet also make flavorful the spices that you have. For if you had no eyes you could be excused, but you do have eyes, therefore why do you not look around yourself, thanks to them? Yet you have ready discourse in your rationality. Indeed, many times you judge others in matters in which you do not wish yourself to be judged, and still sometimes you say wisely what you express. Take care to carry your burden and collect every good work in the purse of your heart lest you lack any of them, for in the solitary life that you seek according to your wishes, you will not be able to find rest in the midst of new, difficult conditions, unknown to you, indeed worse than the ones before, and also heavier, as it is with the casting of a stone. So, imitate the turtle-dove in chastity, yet carefully select a choice vineyard so that you might see God with an upright and pure aspect."

In other words, Hazzecha was tempted to leave the monastery for a solitary life, and Hildegard advised her to see to her current situation rather than expose herself to new difficulties which would arise for her in solitude, leading to a still-worse state than the one she was suffering from. Hazzecha undoubtedly displayed some degree of instability, at least interiorly, against which Hildegard was warning her. It is also likely that another letter (not published in the Patrology yet reproduced by Peter Dronke) comes from the same Hazzecha, who was thinking either about leading a solitary life or else making a pilgrimage to Rome. Hildegard again placed her on guard against this instability that could only harm her. She urged her to ask God for holy discretion:

> O daughter of God, you who call this poor little woman to be a mother in the love of God, learn to have discretion, which in heaven and on earth is the mother of all things, since thanks to it the soul is ruled and the body nourished in healthy austerity.

On several occasions in other correspondence, Hildegard comes back to this discretion to which one must recur in all things, and particularly to avoid excesses of penance and mortification which in reality are errors, "diabolical errors." She is able to find image-laden accents to convince and soothe her correspondents. She writes to the abbess of Saint Mary's in Ratisbon:

> Oh! Imitate the dove in its piety when your spirit restlessly seeks to understand many things, which you cannot attain; thus keep yourself at rest and learn moderation, for the dove is also moderate and stable. When a vehement rage drains you, look at the pure source of patience, and soon that rage will abate and the storm will pass as will the wave of impetuous ardor, for the dove is patience. . . . Live according to the dove's example, and you will live for eternity.

To another in whom she perceives some excessive privations, she recommends:

Take care that you hold your ground in solitude and that you not ruin it in such a way that the greenness [vigor] of herbs and the spices of virtues cannot grow there, worn as they are by the plow that tills them. I often see [she adds] that when someone afflicts one's body by an excess of abstinence, that disgust arises in one, and through disgust vices multiply much more than if they had been restrained with balance.

Similar counsels of moderation recur many times in her letters.

CHAPTER V

THE EMPEROR AND THE NUN

WHEN WE STUDY HILDEGARD'S correspondence as the Patrology edition transmits it to us, we see a hierarchical classification of letters received or sent: first, popes and bishops; next—something surprising in the case of a nun—political authorities, beginning with the emperors of Germany. Then come important people in secular life such as the count of Flanders, then the abbots of monasteries, provosts, priests, simple monks, etc., and also a certain number of untitled correspondents, simple people who ask for her advice or plead for her prayers.

The first of these letters issuing from a temporal authority is addressed to her by the emperor Conrad III of Hohenstaufen. Although absorbed thoroughly by his high office and by the different cares and petitions besetting him, he nonetheless had to write to her, because he had learned about the holiness of her life and that she had been visited by the Holy Spirit. He assured her of his goodwill toward her and her sisters; in any way possible, he would provide them aid in any situation; he earnestly sought their prayers for himself and for his son whom he hoped, he said, would survive him. In fact this son, Henry, did not survive him, and it was to his nephew Frederick that Conrad left his empire when he died on February 15, 1152.

His succession, moreover, was not arranged by that date, and he could only recommend to the prince electors this nephew promised to a glorious and stormy reign.

It is through a letter from Frederick, the new emperor himself, that we learn that Hildegard was invited by him to come and see him in his palace at Ingelheim. "We are informing your holiness," he writes, "that what you foretold when we, while residing at Ingelheim, had asked you to come into our presence, we now have in our hands." Such an audience deserved to pass into History. The emperor Frederick was none other than the one whom we know under the name of Frederick Barbarossa. Elected on March 4, 1152, at Frankfurt, he was crowned on the ninth of the same month at Aix-la-Chapelle, and it is probable that this visit took place at the beginning of his accession to the head of the empire, perhaps in that very year of 1152. The Patrology edition preserves only a single exchange of letters, that of the emperor Frederick partially quoted, and Hildegard's answer, but the writers of her *Life* do not speak of any episode that would have deserved to keep their attention.

It is indeed difficult to imagine a more complete contrast than between her who describes herself as a *paupercula femina,* a poor and miserable woman, a *paupercula forma,* a poor and miserable figure, a little feather supported by the wind that carries her where it wills (this is her favorite image for designating herself), and the magnificent emperor destined to enter into legend as well as into history, who summoned her. He was about thirty years old, solidly built, robust, with hair and beard a reddish blond that earned him his surname Barbarossa (Redbeard); courageous, avid for glory as much as for justice, and already famous for the exploits that he had carried out in the East. He had indeed joined the expedition, some six years earlier, that was intended to relieve Jerusalem at the appeal of Queen Melisende; the expedition did not achieve the expected results, but during it Frederick's exploits marked him for the attention of other crusaders.

The audience between the young and magnificent emperor and the little nun, who was beset by premature infirmities that did not cease to threaten her existence, took place in the superb setting of the palace of Ingelheim, near Mainz, one of the rare imperial palaces whose modern excavations have enabled the finding of some vestiges. It had already been described by an ninth-century poet, Ermold the Black, in a poem dedicated to the emperor Louis the Pious, the son of Charlemagne. He speaks of it as "an immense palace, supported on one hundred columns, abounding in passages and in structures of all sorts, doors, recesses, innumerable rooms." It was decorated with many paintings, which in the chapel invoked "the illustrious acts of God"—in other words, scenes from the Old and New Testaments—and in the royal hall they invoked "lofty human deeds," the exploits of the sovereigns of Antiquity and those of Charlemagne himself; this doubtlessly referred to mosaics with gold background, such as those that some Italian churches have preserved up till our times, in Venice for example, or also the church of Germigny-des-Prés in France.

This was truly a sumptuously adorned place, which served as a setting for the encounter between the red-bearded emperor and the frail and inspired religious. She without doubt warned her imperial host about certain dangers threatening him, against which she invited him to keep his guard, since in his letter he strives to inform her about this matter: "We do not cease in any way to work with all our effort for the honor of the realm." He then assures her that with regard to the temporal affairs that she discussed with him, he intends to judge them with the most complete equity, "not allowing himself to be swayed either by friendship or by hate toward anyone, but only by respect for justice."

Hildegard's answer shows her to be hardly intimidated by the stature of her correspondent. "The little feather upheld by the wind" sends him the words that she has heard, she states, from the supreme Judge. She first notes that it is striking that "you who are king, you regard this person as necessary." And she continues, in a process that is common in her correspondence as in her works, by developing an image:

Listen: a king was standing on a high mountain and was looking into every valley to see what each one was doing in them . . . and watching so that what was arid might become green, what was sleeping might awake. . . . When that man ceased keeping his eye open, a black cloud came up that covered the valleys. Soon crows and other birds rushed down. . . . At this time, O king, watch with care since all your regions are darkened by the false mob of those who destroy justice in the foulness of their faults. . . . You who are king, with your scepter of mercy rule the lazy, the wayward, those of cruel behavior. You truly have a glorious name, for you are king in Israel; very glorious is your name. See, then, that the supreme King is looking at you, lest you be accused of not having performed your duties justly, and lest you have reason for shame over them. That would not be pleasing to God!

She exhorts him to watch over the behavior of prelates who lapse into carelessness and abjectness.

Shun that, O king; be the soldier, the armed knight, courageously fight the demon, so that you might not be routed and that your earthly kingdom have nothing to suffer thereby. . . . Reject avarice, choose abstinence, which the King of kings truly loves. For it is very necessary for you to be prudent on every occasion. I do indeed see you, in a mystical vision, living in all sorts of troubles and nuisances in the eyes of your contemporaries; yet nonetheless you will have, for the term of your reign, what is suitable for earthly affairs. Be on guard, then, lest the Sovereign King cast you down to the ground as a consequence of the blindness of your eyes that do not see rightly as you hold in your hand the scepter of your reign. Let not, then, the grace of God be lacking to you.

Such a letter foretells both the length of Barbarossa's reign and the troubles he would face, for which uprightness and prudence would be necessary.

The tone of this correspondence could only change afterward, with the resumption of the conflict between the Church and the empire, with instances of violence, as when Frederick deposed the archbishop of Mainz who remained faithful to Rome, or when his troops razed the city of Milan. There were no less than four antipopes named by the emperor during the pontificate of Alexander III.

Hildegard would not see the unexpected end of Barbarossa, who drowned in Armenia, in the waters of the Self, at the beginning of the new Crusade that he had undertaken to try to liberate Jerusalem, fallen once again into Saladin's hands. This abrupt end of the great emperor occurred in 1190, when the abbess had already been dead for eleven years.

Hildegard was consulted by still another powerful personage on the matter of the Crusade. This was Philip of Alsace, count of Flanders. His letter unfortunately cannot be dated, except by the very title Philip of Flanders; it was not until 1168 that he succeeded his father Thierry, yet he was, as was often done, associated with the government of the county since 1157. He had to have written before September 1177, the time when he set out definitively for the Holy Land and disembarked in Acre with an outstanding retinue of knights. It is known that for a long time he hesitated before undertaking the journey to Jerusalem—

and it is evidently during this period of hesitation that he wrote to Hildegard. It is significant to see how this powerful prince addresses the abbess from the banks of the Rhine.

Philip, count of Flanders and of Vermandois, to Maid Hildegard, servant of Christ, health and great affection.

Your holiness must have known that I am ready to do everything within my power to please you, for your holy conversation and your upright life have very often resounded in my ears in praise of you. Although I am sinful and unworthy, nonetheless with all my heart I love the servants and friends of Christ and I gladly honor them with all veneration, remembering what Scripture says: "The urgent prayer of the just has great worth." This is why I am sending to the favor of your kindness the bearer of these present letters, a very faithful servant who will speak with you for me, a miserable sinner; I would nonetheless have preferred to come to you and talk with you as I wished, but my concerns are so numerous and so great, arising every day, that I could not put them aside for that purpose. Indeed, the time is coming when I must set out for Jerusalem; this is why a great work of preparation is upon me, concerning which please send me your counsel in your letters. I believe indeed that the renown of my name has often reached you as well as that of my deeds, and I have need, for much among them, of the mercy of God. This is why I ask you and plead with you, in very great earnestness of prayer, that you might intercede with the Lord for me, so wretched and

tempered man, cruel in his revenge. She then moves on to more direct advice.

> Listen at this time, O son of God, so that you might be able to look toward God with the pure eye of justice as the eagle looks at the sun, so that your judgments might be just and purged of your own will, lest it not be said to you by the supreme Just One who has given his precept to man, who appeals to him through penance in his mercy, that he will not say to you: "Why have you killed your neighbor without my justice intervening?"

This sentence is very striking when we learn that Philip had had a man killed under the whip; his name was Gautier de Fontaines, and he had been found in conversation with the count's wife. Hildegard continues by saying to him a little afterward:

> Thus, take all your instances of neglect and your faults and your unjust judgments, take refuge with the sign of the cross toward the living God who is the Way and the Truth and who says: "I do not wish the death of the sinner, but rather that he convert and live." And if the time comes when the infidels dedicate themselves to destroying the fountain of faith, then resist them as much as you can with the help of God's grace. For me, I see in my soul that the distress that you have in your anxieties of your soul is like the dawn that arises in the morning. Then, may the Holy Spirit work in you through pure and

true repentance and make of it a flaming sun so that you might seek him, that you might serve him alone, and that you might live in eternity in complete beatitude.

The rest of the story proves that Hildegard's reservations were justified. Indeed, Count Philip would gravely disappoint those who, in the Holy Land, were awaiting his arrival.

In 1177, people did not know that the end of the kingdom of Jerusalem was so near—it would fall ten years later into Saladin's hands—but it was strongly felt that this kingdom was precarious. The king of Jerusalem then was the young Baldwin IV, still an adolescent, but in whom the progress of leprosy was becoming evident, leaving him little hope for survival and even less for offspring. Two years earlier he had given in marriage his sister Sybille, for whom the kingdom was destined, to the Piedmontese prince Guillaume Longue-Épée, the son of the marquis of Montferrat, thus hoping to assure dynastic succession. Now Guillaume, carried away by an epidemic illness, had died in June 1177. The arrival of the count of Flanders at the head of a shining army thus represented a great hope for the barons of the Holy Land. Soon, King Baldwin offered him the "baylie," the guard of the kingdom, but— one hears it upon reading the question posed by Philip to Hildegard—the latter's resolution was far from being set. He refused. He had also refused to take part in an expedition planned against Egypt together with Byzantine forces;

such an expedition would probably have stopped the rising
star of Saladin, in whom they perceived an enemy who
would not delay in winning, yet Philip of Flanders did not
want to be in it. Finally, the Byzantine fleet, gathered in the
harbor of Acre, allowed itself incessant delays which divided it, and went back to sea without having fought.

Philip of Flanders, his pilgrimage over, finished by lend-
ing a helping hand in Syria, in the valley of Oronte, before
returning to the West and leaving behind him a very dis-
tressing situation. Only the bravery of the young leprous
king who, attacked by Saladin with forces ten times larger
in number, achieved against all expectation the famous victory of Montgisard, would assure for nearly ten years the
survival of the kingdom. As for Philip, seized by late
remorse, he returned to the Holy Land fourteen years later
and died outside Saint John of Acre on June 1, 1191; the
sun perceived in him by Hildegard had been slow to rise!

One suspects that she uses a completely different tone
when she addresses Saint Bernard—for Bernard of
Clairvaux in person wrote to the abbess of Bingen, and he
even excused himself for too short a letter.

I am in haste to write to the sweetness of your devout charity,
although surely more briefly than I would prefer, since I have
many matters I must attend to. [He continues:] We thank the
grace of God that is in you and that you hold as a grace, and
we counsel you to strive to respond to it with all the effort of
your humility and of your devotion. [Later he adds:] This is

why we again pray and we ask in a pleading manner that you call us to mind before God along with all those joined with us in spiritual companionship. . . . Indeed, we pray assiduously for you, so that you might be strengthened in the good, instructed in interior matters, and that you continue to make progress toward those that endure.

To this letter, Hildegard responds with a very lovely missive, in which she allows herself to go a bit into what one might call confidences.

. . . I, wretched and more than wretched, in my name of woman since my childhood, I have seen great marvels that my tongue cannot utter, although it is nothing else than what the Holy Spirit teaches in the manner that I can say them. O Father, sure and gentle, listen to me, your unworthy servant, in your kindness, I who have never lived in security since my childhood. In your piety and your wisdom, understand in your soul according as you have received from the Holy Spirit, since the things that have been said to you by me are of this nature: indeed, I know in their text the interior understanding of what the psalms, the Gospel, and other volumes present to us, which are shown to me in this vision that touches my heart and burns my soul as a flame, teaching me about what there is of depth in these works. Nevertheless, this does not teach me the letters of the German language that I do not know. I simply know how to read in simplicity, not in the precision of the text, for I am ignorant, not having had any instruction of an exterior kind, but it is at the interior, in my soul, that I am taught. So I speak to you, because I have no doubt about you, but I feel consoled by your wisdom and by your piety in that there are many errors among men, by what I hear said about them.

And she tells that she has first opened her "secrets," as she says, to a monk who has encouraged and reassured her. She continues:

I wish, Father, that for the love of God you remember me in your prayers. Two years ago, I saw you in this vision as a man looking at the sun, with no fear, but with great boldness, and I wept because I am timid and lack boldness. Kind and gentle Father, place me in your soul, pray for me, for I have great sufferings in this vision, so that I might tell what I see and what I hear.

Then, recalling the infirmities by which she is often overwhelmed, she turns again to Saint Bernard and says to him:

For you, you are the eagle looking at the sun.

She asks him to consider her words and concludes:

I ask you to place them in your heart so that you do not cease . . . to look upon God for me, since God wants you for himself in your soul, and be strong in God amid struggles. Amen.

After seeing Hildegard invited by the emperor and receiving

a letter from Saint Bernard, who was certainly the highest spiritual authority of his age, we are not surprised at finding her in correspondence with the popes of that period, those who succeeded Eugene III, from whom she received such a striking confirmation of her visions and her writings. His successor, Anastasius IV, addresses her in the most admiring terms:

> We rejoice in the Lord and we are gladdened that the name of Christ is glorified in you day after day. . . . We have indeed heard and seen many things about you. [He mentions that he is aware that his predecessor in the see of Saint Peter held her in affection:] Following his steps, we wish to write to you and we desire a response from you, for we seek what God has done in you, although we only limp toward the good things we long for, out of weariness of body as well as of spirit. . . .

Without doubt he did not expect the response that the abbess of Bingen gave him:

> O personage who are the eminent defense and summit of authority of the ornate city that is instituted as the Bride of Christ, listen to her who has not begun to live, but who does not allow herself to be cast down by what is lacking to her. O man, who in regard to your knowledge have grown weary of quelling prideful boasting among people placed under your protection, why do you not revive the castaways who cannot escape their hardships unless they receive help? And why do

you not cut the root of evil that chokes the good and useful herbs that have a sweet taste and pleasant odor? You neglect the king's daughter, namely justice, beloved by higher powers and entrusted to you. You allow that this daughter of the king be cast down to the ground, that the diadem and ornament of her tunic be ravaged by the coarseness of strange customs of those men who bark in the manner of dogs and, in the manner of roosters who try to sing sometimes in the night, emit a silly sound with their voice. These are the pretenders who speak of peace falsely, but among themselves they gnash their teeth in their hearts, just like the dog that greets with a wag of its tail the companions that it knows, but bites with sharp teeth the honest soldier who is helpful in the king's house. . . .

The letter continues in this tone, capable of leaving its addressee dumbfounded. She also does not fear the threats that allow terrible future times to be foreseen:

Listen now to him who lives and who will see no end: "The world is at present in cowardice, then it will be in sadness, later in terror to the point that people will not dread being killed. In all this there is sometimes the moment of impudence, sometimes the moment of contrition, and sometimes the moment of lightning and thunder of various iniquities. . . ."

And Hildegard concludes with vivid exhortations:

Therefore, O man, since you seem to have been constituted

shepherd, get up and run more rapidly toward justice lest before the supreme Physician you be accused of not having cleansed your sheepfold of its filth and of not having anointed it with oil. . . . Therefore, man, stay on the right path and you will save yourself so that he will lead you in the way of blessing and election, and you will live for eternity.

Anastasius IV had only a very brief pontificate, from July 1153 to December 1154. With the reading of Hildegard's letter, it seems that Christianity need not have mourned this brevity. Adrian IV, his successor, was the only pope of English origin in the annals of the Church. Capable and energetic, he was a friend of John of Salisbury, the famous scholar who was bishop of Chartres. As his predecessor had done, he addressed Hildegard in the most laudatory terms: "We rejoice, my daughter, and we exult in the Lord that the fame of your virtue has spread far and wide so that for many you are like a perfume of life for life and that the multitude of faithful people cry out their praise for you." He urges her to persevere:

Think, then, my daughter, that the serpent who caused man to lose paradise wishes to snatch those who are important like Job. . . . And since you know that many are called but few are chosen, be part of the small number of those chosen, so as to persevere until the end in this framework, and instruct your sisters, entrusted to your wisdom, in the works of salvation through which, with them, you can, with the help of the Lord, attain him whom eye has not seen nor ear heard, and who has not come down to the human heart. We wish to receive from you in response some words of recommendation, for it is said that you are imbued with God's spirit of miracles, over which we rejoice greatly and give to you the glory of divine grace.

Hildegard's answer is completely different in tone than the one she sent to Anastasius IV. She addresses someone who has harsh combats to undergo. She warns him that he will have dealings with people who behave like bears and leopards:

But the sword of God will slay them so that among them a good leader will rise up. For now, I recommend that you impose a rein on those who are subject to you, and not to allow them to speak evil against you. . . . Watch, then, with zeal over what the state of people's morals in these times requires. O gentle Father, remember that you are a man on earth and do not fear that God will neglect you, for you will see his light.

Regarding Alexander III, his pontificate that began in 1159 showed itself to be difficult as well, since the throne of Saint Peter was disputed between two pretenders—some even wanted to resort to the arbitration of the emperor Frederick Barbarossa! Four antipopes would follow, one of whom would canonize Charlemagne—a straightforward way to pay his respects to the reigning emperor. The latter did not reconcile with the pope until 1177. As for Hildegard, when she was passing through a difficult period, she wrote to the pontiff to plead for his help. Alexander III turned to the provost of Saint Andrew in Cologne to settle the dispute and provide the requested relief to the abbess.

Suffice to say that all the mighty, everyone who counted in the temporal and spiritual world, are found in Hildegard's correspondence. We will return to the number and variety of these correspondents in connection with her preaching. To close this chapter, it is not without interest to mention the letters that she exchanged with another mystic, also German—Elizabeth of Schönau.

Elizabeth seems to have possessed the gift of prophecy, but she found herself exposed to mockery by certain clerics, who twisted her words. She writes to Hildegard,

I confess having conceived some clouds of disturbance in the soul, recently, because of the foolish remarks of people who say many things in my regard, which are not true. Yet I would easily put up with the remarks of the crowd if those who walk about in religious habits did not grieve my spirit even more deeply. For among them, stirred by whatever zeal, there are those who turn into derision the grace of God that is in me and who are not afraid to judge rashly on things they know nothing about. I hear it said that some present, here and there, some letters written in their spirit under my own name. They defame me, saying that I have prophesied on the subject of the day of the Judgment, which I surely would never have had the presumption to do, since that event escapes the knowledge of all mortals.

She adds that, in order to avoid any arrogance, as much as she can, she keeps hidden everything taught to her by revelation. But she heard herself vehemently reproached by an angel for hiding the word of God told to her, "not for it to be hidden, but for it to be manifested for the praise and glory of Our Lord and for the salvation of souls around her."

There follows a kind of review of this revelation concerning the imminent Judgment, which was made to her at very precise times. On the feast of Saint Barbara, during Advent, she shared it with the abbot of a monastery, who himself spoke about it to prelates of the Church and to different people of religion,

some of whom received it only with respect, others, however, very differently, and they spoke of it in a disagreeable manner. It was found that many among those who heard talk about this word did penance during the whole time of Lent, in great fear, and made use of alms and prayers. . . . On the fourth weekday [Wednesday] before Easter, after great corporal sufferings, I was seized in ecstasy and the angel of the Lord appeared to me and I said to him: "Lord, what about the word that you addressed to me?" He answered: "Do not be afflicted, do not be troubled, if the things that I foretold to you have not happened on the day that I indicated to you, for the Lord has been appeased by the satisfactions that many have offered to him." After that, on the sixth weekday [Friday], toward the third hour [nine o'clock in the morning], I fell into great suffering in going out of myself and again he stood before me, saying: "The Lord has seen the affliction of his people and he has turned away from them the wrath of his indignation." I answered: "What then, Lord, will I not be scorned by many of those to whom this word was extended?" He said: "Whatever happens to you on this occasion, bear it patiently and with goodwill; keep in mind that the Creator of the entire universe has borne the mockery of men. For now, God is testing your patience."

In ending, Elizabeth of Schönau adds:

See, I have revealed to you, lady, the whole thing in order, so that you might know my innocence and that of the abbot who is concerned for me, and so that you might make it known to others. I ask you to have me share in your prayers and, according as the Spirit of God suggests to you, to send me some consolations. The grace of Christ be with you.

Hildegard's response is at the level of the trust that Elizabeth shows for her. She begins by specifying, as she often does, that nothing comes from her, but from the "serene light," since she is but a "wretched vessel of clay."

And, in accordance with the method that is her own, she begins by setting everything in the order of creation:

> Herbs, plants, and trees appeared; the sun as well, the moon and the stars advance in their order and the fish in the water and the fowl appeared. . . . But, while God prepared great knowledge for man, man stood up in his own spirit and turned away from God. . . . O misfortune, then all the elements were embroiled in the difficulties of light and darkness, so that man went into transgression of God's precepts. . . . This was up to the time that the Word of God appeared, as the sun of justice advanced and illuminated men with his good works in faith and in works while the dawn appears first and the other hours of the day follow until nightfall; and see, my daughter Elizabeth, how the world finds itself changed.

And humans suffer the seduction of the ancient serpent:

> When this same serpent sees a valuable gem, immediately it howls, saying: "What is this?" And it makes its spirit suffer all sorts of miseries, desirous of flying above the clouds. . . . Listen now: those who wish to accomplish the works of God must always comprehend that they are vessels of clay. . . . The one who is of heaven while others are distant from it does not know the heavenly things, but sings the secrets of God; just as a trumpet that only produces sounds does not play itself, but when another breathes inside it, it produces sound. Let those then put on the breastplate of faith, the gentle, the merciful,

the poor and the wretched, as was this Lamb, who himself issues the sound of the trumpet.

She finishes by urging Elizabeth to patience and to joy:

O my daughter, may God make of you a mirror of life. As for me, who remains in the fright of fear, sometimes only in sounding a bit like a little sound of a trumpet under the action of the living Light, may God help me to remain in his service.

Each one could understand the other, aware that they were receiving everything from God in the poverty of their personal being.

CHAPTER VI

UNIVERSE AND MAN
IN HILDEGARD'S VISIONS

IN THE MANUSCRIPT THAT the *Biblioteca governativa* preserves at Lucca, two full-page miniatures draw attention: they represent a man, arms extended, standing out from the circle that symbolizes the world. Quite curiously, this image has become familiar; it has even been somewhat debased, having served in advertising for a company (Manpower)—at least under a much more recent form, due to Leonardo da Vinci.

More than three centuries before the latter's birth, this vision of man, arms extended over the globe of the earth, was present in the work of the little nun from the banks of the Rhine. But while Leonardo da Vinci has been studied, explored, extolled, and widely diffused in classic and modern times, the work of Hildegard, and her era in general, have been forgotten and unrecognized. The fact remains that this image which places man in the center of the universe was familiar since the twelfth century, and summarizes what Hildegard reveals to us about the cosmos.

Without doubt the essence of her work—in any case, what she has that is most striking—is there, in this view of the world through her visions. She expresses herself on this topic especially in her third work, the one that can be considered her most finished, most complete, most striking as well, *Le Livre des oeuvres divines (The Book of Divine Works)*. It is fortunately within our reach today, thanks to the magnificent labor of Bernard Gorceix. We will make mention here only of the principal of these cosmic visions that reveal to us a universe totally acceptable with respect to the discoveries of our times — especially if one thinks about the concept of a closed and limited universe, which reigned from the sixteenth century up until the nineteenth. We will not attempt further to clarify the scientific implications that these visions can possess; they are expressed in a totally different register than that of pure science; their originality, their poetic power, make them by themselves captivating, and suffice, we believe, to arouse interest.

Le Livre des oeuvres divines opens on a sumptuous image that has recently been reproduced several times, that of a person standing, possessing three heads and four wings painted in shades of scarlet. This image is accompanied by a commentary that must be quoted in order to introduce the work and thus penetrate the set of visions that she unfolds.

I then contemplated in the secret of God, at the heart of airy spaces in the middle, a marvelous figure. Its face was so beautiful and bright that looking at the sun was easier than looking at that face. A large golden circle surrounded the head. In the circle a second face, that of an old man, rose over the first; its chin and its beard grazed the peak of the head. On each side of the neck of the first figure a wing projected. These wings lifted up and joined above the golden circle. The outside part of the right wing's curve bore an eagle's head; from its fiery eyes glistened angelic splendor as in a mirror. The corresponding part of the left wing bore a man's head that shone like twinkling stars. These two faces were turned toward the east. From each shoulder of the figure, a wing hung down to the knees. A vestment as bright as the sun covered it. In its hands it carried a lamb which shone like a day flooded with light. On foot, it was treading on a monster of frightful appearance, foul and black, and a serpent. The serpent was clasping in its jaws the monster's right ear. Its body coiled around the monster's head, and its tail reached down to its feet, on the figure's left side.

The figure spoke in these words: "I am the supreme energy, the fiery energy. I am the one who inflamed each spark of life. Nothing that is mortal flows in me. I decide on every reality. My upper wings envelop the earthly circle; in wisdom, I am the universal orderer. Fiery life of essential being: since God is intellect, how could he not act? Through man, he assures the unfolding of all his works. Indeed, he created man in his image and in his likeness; in him he inscribed, with steadfastness and measure, the totality of creatures. From all eternity, the creation of this work—the creation of man—was foreseen in his counsel. Once this work is achieved, he then places in man's hands the whole of creation, so that man can act with it in the same manner that God had fashioned his work, man. So then, I am servant and support. Through me all life is indeed inflamed. Without origin, without end, I am that life that remains the same and eternal. This life is God. It is perpetual movement, perpetual operation, and its unity is shown in a triple energy. Eternity is the Father; the Word is the Son; the breath that binds the two is the Holy Spirit. God has represented it in man; man indeed has a body, a soul, and an intellect. My flames dominate the beauty of the countryside: the earth is the matter thanks to which God fashioned man. If I penetrate the waters by my light, it is that the soul penetrates the whole body, just as water by its flow penetrates the whole earth. If I say that I am ardor in the sun and in the moon, it is an allusion to intellect: are the stars not innumerable words of intelligence? And if my breath, invisible life, universal protector, awakens the universe to life, it involves a symbol: the air and the wind indeed support everything that grows and ripens, and nothing is taken away from the gifts of its nature."

I then heard the same voice. From heaven it spoke to me in these words: "God, the creator of the universe, fashioned man in his image and in his likeness. In him, he represented every creature, higher and lower. He loved him with such a love that he reserved for him the place from which he had expelled the fallen angel. He granted him all the glory, all the honor that this angel had lost at the same time as his salvation. See what the face that you are contemplating shows to you. The magnificent figure that you perceive in the midst of airy spaces and in the secret of God, and whose appearance is human, indeed symbolizes that love of the Father of heaven. It is love: within the energy of the everlasting deity, in the mystery of his gifts, it is a marvel of outstanding beauty. If it has human appearance, it is because the Son of God was clothed in flesh, to rescue man from perdition in the service of love. This is why the face has such beauty and brightness. This is why it would be easier for you to contemplate the sun rather than contemplate this face. The profusion of love indeed is radiant, the gleam of a brilliance so sublime and so blazing that it surpasses in a way inconceivable to our senses every act of human understanding that enables normally in the soul the understanding of the most diverse subjects. We will show them here by a symbol, which allows us to recognize in faith what the outer eyes cannot really contemplate."

Hildegard opens her visions with the Holy Trinity: Eternity, Word, Breath are represented here, signifying that God is Life and that he is Love. The supreme energy, the fiery energy, has brought about the creation of man, who is born as body, soul, spirit. Everything proceeds from this life, liberating a triple energy of love of which man is a reflection. The whole is expressed with a liveliness, with a sense of beauty of which the visionary underlines that it stands at the limit of what man can contemplate. She herself, in the frame where she is depicted under the full-page image, turns toward the vision with eyes in ecstasy.

A second evocation expands on the first. It is both more complex and more detailed. Returning to the trinitarian image and the "vision in the form of an egg" that she had developed in her first work, the *Scivias*, Hildegard describes the man at the center of the world. This she does with rigorous precision: The man is situated at the center of a series of circles, the first of black fire, the second clear, and twice as wide as the first; inside, a circle of humidity, under which appears another, white and dense; six circles thus form a kind of giant wheel around the man.

Within the figure's chest that I had contemplated in the midst of the airy spaces in the middle, there appeared a wheel of marvelous appearance. It contained signs that compared with the vision in the form of an egg that I had twenty-eight years ago, and that I described in the third vision of my book *Scivias*. Under the curve of the shell and in the upper part a circle of clear fire appeared that dominated another of black fire. These two circles were united as if they only formed one. Under the black one there appeared one that resembled pure ether, as thick as the first two joined together. Then there came a circle that was like air filled with humidity, as wide as the one of luminous fire. Under this circle of humid air appeared another of white, dense air, the hardness of which recalls that of a human tendon; it had the same width as the one of black fire. These two circles were also bound to each other as if they formed only one. Finally, under this white and firm air, a second airy layer showed itself, a thin one, which seemed to spread over the whole circle, appearing to raise clouds, some light, some low and dark. These six circles were bound to each other without intermediate spaces. The upper circle flooded the other spheres with its light, although the one of watery air permeated all the others with its humidity.

The figure of the man occupied the center of this giant wheel. The head was above and the feet were touching the sphere of dense, white and shining air. The fingers of both hands, right and left, were extended in the form of a cross, in the direction of the circumference, the arms likewise.

This whole vision is shaken by gusts that emanate from four groups of animal heads: leopard, wolf, lion, bear; then crab, stag, serpent, lamb.

Above the head of this figure stood the seven planets: three in the circle of the fire of light, one in the sphere of black fire, three in the circle of pure ether. All the planets shone in the direction of the animals' heads and of the figure of the man. . . . The circle of luminous fire encompassed sixteen principal stars, four between the heads of the leopard and the lion, four between those of the wolf and the lion, four between those of the wolf and the bear, four between those of the bear and of the leopard. Eight of them occupied an intermediate position, and they aided one another: they were situated between the heads and they sent their rays to one another, which hit the layer of thin air. The eight others, beside the other animals' heads, hit with their rays the clouds that spread out facing them. On the right side of the image, two tongues, distinct from one another, formed something like two streams that poured upon the wheel and the human figure. It also went upon the left side: it was like foam.

As one can see, the universe described here is in no way static; actions and interactions are opposed, and indeed balance one another, just as the fiery energy is tempered by the humid circle. Above all, winds go all around it; the lion's head is a symbol of the southern wind, the main one, accompanied by two winds connected to the heads of the serpent and the lamb. These winds

> maintain the energy of the entire universe and of the man, both of which harbor the totality of the creature. They protect them from destruction; the connected winds for their part blow constantly, albeit softly, like zephyrs. The terribly powerful energies of the main winds are not required. They will not be so until the Judgment of God, at the end of the world, so that the final punishment can be carried out. . . . The southern wind brings the dog days and provokes great floods, the northern wind brings lightning and thunder, hail and cold.

In the course of the text, the passions that shake humans are themselves compared to the winds. When a wind begins to blow, whether naturally or in virtue of a divine command, it penetrates the body of the man with nothing to stop it, and the soul, taking it in, guides it naturally toward the interior to the members of the body, whichever they may be, that correspond to its nature. Thus its gust both comforts and frustrates the man.

After enumerating everything that in nature influences, as well the latter, the sun, the moon, the planets, Hildegard has a reflection for the man himself.

> As for you, man, who see this spectacle, understand that these

phenomena likewise concern the interior of the soul.

These interactions of natural elements and of human tendencies are found in other works of Hildegard that are strictly medical in character. She pushes her comparisons here quite far.

To the four principal winds correspond the four energies within man: thought, word, intention, and affective life. Just as each wind can send its gust toward the right or toward the left, so also the soul armed with these four energies can, through natural science, attain the part that it desires in choosing either good or evil.

And it can compare to the southern wind, the one that brings the warmth, "the good and holy thoughts that the zeal of a pious intention stirs up, thanks to the fire of the Holy Spirit." In contrast, the western wind, which is cold, "indicates the dishonest and useless thoughts which the fire of the Holy Spirit does not warm, cold and dishonest works." Only the northern wind "is useless for every creature. It also has two wings, the one turned toward the east, the other toward the west. They indicate in man that knowledge of Good and that knowledge of Evil thanks to which he considers, in his soul, as in a mirror, what is useful and what is useless. In the same way, the firmament, upper and lower, rules the earth."

These visions as a whole place the accent on a kind of cosmic unity that rules or that influences both man and the world in which he lives. Thus the Aquilo, the northern wind, "is a dangerous wind; it is harmful to everything that it touches. Its cold and its harshness touch both the warm gust that comes down gently from the sun in dropping dew, and that brings forth on the earth all the greenness of the fruits of the fields." Here we touch upon one of Hildegard's favorite notions, greenness or viridity, from the Latin *viriditas,* green, vigorous; it applies equally to nature and to man, designating that inner energy that makes plants grow and by which man develops.

Hildegard emphasizes,

All these phenomena relate to the soul. The soul indeed is present in the body as a wind which one neither sees nor hears blowing. Like the air, it spreads its puff after the manner of the wind, its sighs and its thoughts; its humidity bearer of its good intentions toward God, makes it like the dew. Like the glow of the sun that sheds light on the whole world and that never weakens, the soul is entirely present in the small form of man. Its thoughts allow it to fly in every direction: holy works lift it toward the stars for the praise of God, while the evil works of sins hurl it down into the darkness.

She continues by detailing the fourth vision:

The rational soul utters many words that resound, just as a tree multiplies its branches and, in the same way that the branches come out of the tree, the energies of the man flow from the soul. Its works, whatever they may be, achieved in concert with the man, resemble the fruits of a tree. Indeed, the soul has four wings: the senses, knowledge, will, and intellect.

Hildegard's considerations touching upon man within nature lead her to recall the time of Creation.

When God considered man, he was greatly pleased by him: had he not created him in his likeness and after the texture of his image? It fell to man to proclaim by the instrument of his voice of reason all of the divine marvels! For man is the totality of the divine work, and God is known by man, since God has created for him all creatures and since he has granted him in the kiss of true Love and through reason to celebrate him and to praise him; yet he lacked a helpmate who would resemble him. God gave him this helpmate in the mirror that is woman. She too contained the whole human race that would develop in the divine energy: in this energy, he had made the first man. Thus man and woman joined together to accomplish together their work, for man without woman would not be acknowledged as such, and vice-versa. The woman is the work of the man, the man the instrument of feminine consolation, and the two cannot live separated. The man designates the divinity, the woman the humanity of the Son of God.

Thus all of these visions, whether of man or of the cosmos, resemble in profound unity God and his work. This gives them their grand character.

The soul, insofar as it is in the body, hears God because it comes from God, but insofar as it accomplishes its task in creatures, it does not see God. When it leaves the workshop of its body and when it faces God, it will know its nature and its old corporal dependencies. . . . Thus it eagerly awaits this last day of the world, for it has lost this garment which it loves and which is its own body. When it recovers, it will see with the angels the glorious face of God. . . . "The man is the garment that my Son wears in his royal power so that the God of all creation and the Life of life might appear." . . . In the form of the man, that is the totality of his work that God has granted. [Fourth vision.]

Within this universe, wide room is made for the angels. The sixth vision, which is presented under a form markedly different from the preceding ones, is dedicated almost totally to angels. The visionary this time perceives

a great city in the form of a square, enclosed by a wall, with both splendors and shadows, a city also adorned by hills and images. On the city's eastern side stood a large and high mountain of white hard rock that resembled a volcano. At its summit shone a mirror whose brightness and purity seemed to surpass even those of the sun. A dove appeared in this mirror, with its wings spread, ready to fly. This mirror, which was the place of hidden marvels, gave off a glow that rose and spread, within which a great number of mysteries and many forms and figures were displayed. In this splendor in a southern direction appeared a cloud that was white in its upper part and black in its lower. Above this cloud a whole angelic cohort shone. Some radiated like fire, others were all brightness, the third group sparkled like stars.

This city appears after this point in each of the visions. Within its four walls it contains diverse buildings: churches, palaces, columns, ordinary houses, in an order that varies from one image to another. The sixth vision deals above all, as noted, with the role of angels.

The multitude of angels alongside God is, in heaven, a mystery that the light of divinity totally penetrates. It is an obscure mystery for the creature that is man, unless some luminous signs enable it to be known. This multitude has a reason for being that is more tied to God than to humanity. It appears to humans only rarely. Certain angels, however, who are at the service of humans, reveal themselves by signs when it pleases God: it is that God has entrusted different functions to them and has placed them at the service of creatures.

Among these angels, there is the one "who did not want to exist except for himself," Satan, and those who were dragged along in his fall; yet there was above all,

the great angelic cohort, some like fire, others all brightness, the third kind like the stars. The fire angels contain the most intense energy, nothing can weaken them. God has indeed desired that they should contemplate his face unceasingly. The angels that are all brightness are involved in the service of human works that are also works of God: these works of devotion are presented to the angels at the face of God. The angels do not cease to consider them, and they offer to God their sweet perfume by choosing what is helpful and rejecting what is useless. As for the angels that resemble the stars, they suffer with human nature, and they present it to God as a book. They are companions for humans: they speak to them in words of reason according to God's will, with good actions allowing them to celebrate God, and they turn away from evil actions.

In another vision, the seventh, Hildegard returns to "those two orders, that of angels and that of humans," indicating that

God experiences true joy in the celebration of the angels as well as in the holy works of humans. It is true that the angel is constant in the face of God, while man is unstable: thus, as a parallel, the work of man is often deficient; angelic celebration never is.

One of the visions, the fifth, connects with the Apocalypse, which it expressly cites. The description of the principal image is very different in the fifth vision than in the others.

I perceived the earthly circle divided into five sectors, one on the east, another on the west, the third and the fourth on the south and on the north, the fifth in the center. Each of these sectors has the appearance of a bent bow. One of them, the eastern sector, shines brightly, while the west is partially covered with darkness; the southern sector is divided into three zones, two that show punishments and, in the middle, not punishments but rather horrible monsters that give it a dreadful aspect. . . . In the direction of the east, I saw, above the earthly curvature and at a certain height, a red ball surrounded by a sapphire-colored circle. Two wings came out of the right and the left of these balls; they lifted up from both sides and then curved back; they faced each other, and extended to half of the earthly circumference that they encircled. . . . From this ball there went out to the midst of the wings a route over which a luminous star shone.

In the explanations that follow, one grasps that this is the terrestrial globe, here divided into five zones; moreover, the whole is a figure of man. "The earth represents man. . . . Man is led to the salvation of his soul by the five senses that allow him to satisfy all his needs."

Hildegard then relies on the citations of the Apocalypse in order to evoke different ages—that of Adam, that of the flood, that of the expectation of Christ; finally, with the black horse, the age appears that followed the Passion of Christ. Then comes the pale horse, the one who designates the age during which everything that conforms to the law and to the fullness of God's justice will, in a kind of excessive lividity, be held as nothing. . . . In this age, there will be, everywhere, armed combat, the fruits of the earth will vanish, people will die of sudden death, animals will inflict mortal bites on them. The ancient serpent rejoices over these punishments that afflict the man's soul and body; he himself has lost the glory of the heavens, and he would like for man to attain it no longer. . . . The serpent rejoiced and cried out: "Shame on him who made man: the man renounces his own form, he rejects natural love, the love of women." Thus the diabolical seduction gives rise to criminals and seducers, the hate and the crime of the devil, brigands and thieves; but it is in homosexuality that the sin is most impure, the root of all vices. When these sins have accumulated among the nations, the constitution of God's law will be torn, and the Church, like a widow, will be stricken. Princes, nobles, and the wealthy will be exiled by their subjects, they will flee from town to town, the nobility will be wiped out and the rich will become poor. . . . Indeed, the ancient serpent and the other spirits of nothing have lost the beauty of their form, but they have not abandoned the exaltation of their reason.

Hildegard concludes this series of evocations by another reference to the Apocalypse.

"When the time came for the reddening dawn, that is, the time of full justice thanks to my [God's] Son, the ancient serpent, cast down and stunned, said that he had been totally deceived by a woman, by the Virgin. Therefore his fury will flare up against her. . . . But with the aid of the earth, the woman will become free, for my Son received from her the garment of man, my Son who endured a multitude of insults and sufferings so as to confound the serpent."

To end, let us evoke one of the most astonishing visions, the ninth.

I saw . . . turned to the east a figure whose face and feet shone so brightly that my eyes were dazzled by them. Over its white silk robe, it wore a green mantle, richly adorned with the most diverse gems. On its ears a pendant, a necklace on its chest, on its arm rings and jewels of fine gold set with gems. Yet in the center of the region of Septentrio, I perceived a second figure. A strange apparition, standing. In place of the head, a splendor that dazzled me; at the center of its belly, one saw a man's head with gray hair, bearded, and its feet resembled a lion's paws. It had six wings: two came out of the shoulders, went up, went toward the back and joined again, and they overlapped, so to speak, the splendor that we have evoked. Two other wings also set in the shoulders fell back on the nape of the neck. The two remaining ones descended from the hips down to the heels. Its wings sometimes lifted as if they wished to unfold to allow for flying. The whole body of the figure was covered not with feathers but with scales, like a fish. Regarding the wings on the nape of the neck, they bore five mirrors. The upper mirror on the right wing carried the inscription: "Way and truth." The second mirror in the center: "I am the door to all mysteries of God." The mirror at the end of the right wing: "I am the manifestation of all Good." The upper mirror on the left wing: "I am the mirror that reflects the good intentions of the elect." At the end of the wing, above the fifth mirror: "Tell us if it is right, you the people of Israel." The figure turned its back to Aquilo.

A strange vision, in which unexpected figures mingle, such as the personage covered with fish scales, along with very common images such as that of the mirror. It is known that this is a frequent metaphor in the writings of that age. Glass mirrors, an invention of the early Middle Ages, had become widely used in Hildegard's times. They require light and allow the reflection of wisdom, holiness, the face and the features of those whom one admires, giving rise to the use made of it in literature. A German medievalist has counted more than 250 works entitled *Mirrors*.

The explanation of this new vision is given after the description itself. The radiant figure "is the wisdom of true beatitude. . . its white silk robe is the Son of God who is incarnated in the virginal beauty and who embraces humans in the purity and sweetness of his love." Concerning the green mantle that covers the figure of wisdom, the explanation is worth mentioning.

If the mantle is green, adorned with precious stones, it is because wisdom does not reject these external creatures [the animals] whose spirit dies with the flesh, ground and aerial creatures who crawl or who swim: it makes them grow, it preserves them, because they protect man from slavery by assuring him his food. They also carry the ornaments of wisdom: they do not go beyond their nature, in contrast with man who often transgresses the right path reserved for him.

The explanation relating to the other striking figure immediately follows.

At the top of the figure, in the area of the head, if the brightness is stunning and it shines to the point of dazzling you, it is because no living being, as long as the corporal body weighs him down, can see the excellence of the divinity that illumines everything. . . . It is because God is this brightness that has neither beginning nor end. The man's head that you see on the figure's belly is a reminder of the presence in the perfection of divine works of the ancient plan of salvation for man. If the figure has six wings, it is because we work during six days, and it is because during six days man calls upon and celebrates God, placing himself entirely under his protection. The two wings that join together to protect the brightness that we mentioned designate the love of God and the love of neighbor. . . . As for the lower wings, they designate the present and the future. Currently, generations succeed one another. In the future, this will be the advent of a constant and unfailing life; toward the end of the world, this will be announced by a legion of troubles and of wonders that will announce this end like a flight of birds. . . . If the body is covered with scales like a fish and not with feathers like a bird, this is the reason: just as we do not know how fish are born and how they develop, since they are pulled along by flowing waters, so also the Son of God is born in his perfect holiness in a strange nature distinct from that of other humans. In his perfect justice, he led humans to heaven on the outstretched wings of all his good works. . . .

Finally, then, here is the explanation of the mirrors. They are reminders of "the luminaries of different epochs. They are five in number: Abel, Noah, Abraham, Moses, then the Son of God. All five make clear everything that serves humans on the path of truth. Yet it is the Son of God whose Passion has opened the wall of heavenly joys." The same precision is found in other areas of Hildegard's work, notably in her correspondence. The ages are marked for her by these five personages, calling to mind the stages of humanity up to the coming of Christ.

She ends this vision by the word that summarizes her concept of humanity: "Thus, man is the cloister of the marvels of God." An unknown hand, perhaps in the thirteenth century, has recopied this phrase, which resounds as a key of Hildegard's work, at the end of the ninth vision in the manuscript of Lucca: *Homo est clausura mirabilium Dei.*

CHAPTER VII

THE SUBTLETIES OF NATURE

THE WORK OF HILDEGARD OF BINGEN is immense and diverse. We have brought out the most important part: her visions of the universe, man at the center of the created universe, the musical and poetic expression of her seventy symphonies (and even more), the wealth of her correspondence, that gives witness to the trust placed in her by religious authorities as well as by the secular powers of her epoch. More marginal activities should also be included, such as her curious elaboration of a *lingua ignota,* a new language and even a new alphabet that she seems to have wished to fashion, perhaps with the contribution of the religious around her, and which led to rather bizarre imaginings. This activity shows a spirit of invention that can appear odd, gratuitous, indeed a bit futile, but also a taste for research that is very much of her age—that age where in France, Abelard speaks of his studies as a "permanent inquisition." (The term then meant "research" and was not yet tarnished with the connotation that it acquired in the middle of the thirteenth century.)

In this fruitful life, we must also take into account an activity that clearly steps beyond the usual framework of studies and concerns of a life devoted to prayer. Only two medical works are known that were written in the West in the twelfth century: both are works of Hildegard. She compiled a veritable encyclopedia of her age's knowledge in Germany, in the field of natural sciences on the one hand, and in that of medicine on the other. The one and the other are unexpected, we acknowledge, in the work of a visionary and mystic whom we can easily imagine lost in the contemplation of the beyond.

Hardly anything can be compared to this besides the work of another abbess—of Sainte-Odile at Mont-Sion in Alsace—Herrade of Landsberg. A contemporary of Hildegard, she compiled around 1175–1185 an encyclopedia—the first in our literature—that she calls *Garden of Delights (Hortus deliciarum)*. It is a collection of stories, of chronicles, of different extracts drawn as well from the Bible and from the Fathers of the Church as well as from the works of Honorius of Autun or from the study of daily life, provided for the nuns of Sainte-Odile. For example, there is a chapter on the Trinity, that follows the story of the Creation, and on that occasion some topics ranging from astronomy to agriculture, from surveying to road maintenance. It is from this work that historians of medieval techniques have drawn the largest part of their knowledge; the enormous manuscript of 324 leaves contains no less than 336 miniatures.[2] Hildegard's intention, however, goes

[2] A note is needed here: The manuscript of Herrade was destroyed in the burning of the library of Strasbourg at the time of the Franco-Prussian war in 1870; that of Hildegard, which bore the number 1 in the library of Wiesbaden, disappeared during World War II. The progress achieved in the field of armaments in the nineteenth and twentieth centuries had to be paid by heavy losses in scholarly material.

beyond mere description. She establishes relations between productions of nature and those of human beings, and seeks knowledge relative to man, to his balance, and to his health.

Paradoxically, in our era of immense medical progress, of extremely rich discoveries which, at this level of knowledge, involve seemingly irreversible gains, it is without doubt this legacy of Hildegard that contributes the most to making her known. In the current world, Hildegardian medicine has for a long time attracted the public's attention and spurred numerous books. In France, those by Daniel Maurin are the best known.[3]

In Germany and in Switzerland, several books have appeared; a health facility has even been started that uses the methods recommended by Hildegard. There is discussion about opening a similar one in Britain. More generally, associations of the Friends of Hildegard have been founded in a number of places: in Switzerland, in Austria, in Germany, and in America (at the initiative of Bruce Hozeski at Ball State University, Indiana, currently presided by Professor Pozzi Escot). A comprehensive list can be found in the work entitled *Manuel de la médecine de sainte Hildegarde* by Drs. Gottfried Hertzka and Wighard Strehlow.[4]

What first strikes the reader is the extraordinary range, the diversity of knowledge that Hildegard's two works display. The one, entitled *Physica*, contains nine books, of

---

[3] *Sainte Hildegarde, une médecine tombée du ciel*, tome I, la prévention; tome II, les remèdes. (Éditions Saint-Paul, Paris, Fribourg, 1991 and 1992.)
[4] Éditions Résiac.

which four have been published under that same title by Dr. Elisabeth Klein.[5] Four other books (I, II, IV, and IX) have been published to speak only of French editions by Pierre Monat,[6] under the title *Le Livre des subtilités des créatures divines,* which seems to us to suit the work better. It is also given the name *Livre de médecine composée,* or again, *Causae et Curae.*

The whole work amazes us by the knowledge of nature that such works imply. But how could Hildegard acquire such knowledge when she lived mainly within her convent? The answer is obvious in certain cases. Thus she describes the main rivers of the region where she lives: This very certainly and very simply involves personal observation. In the book dedicated to the elements, she makes mention of the Rhine, the Meuse, the Moselle, the Nahe, the Glan, and the Danube: all of these are rivers that she knew, on which she traveled, particularly when she was called to preach in different towns of the empire. She observes that the Nahe has a thoroughly irregular course: "Sometimes it [the river] runs impetuously, sometimes it drifts in torpor. And because it sometimes flows rapidly, it is found quickly blocked and it stops quickly, and thus it digs out its bed and its banks at little depth." It is clear that she has looked at it. She judges the qualities of their respective waters, warning against those of the Rhine, while the water of the

---

[5] Éditions Societé bâloise Hildegarde, 1988.
[6] Éditions Jérôme Millon, Grenoble, 1988.

Meuse "taken in food and drink, and put into contact with a person's flesh in a bath, or used for cleansing the face, renders the person's skin and flesh clear and light." Likewise she indicates that one can use this water for cooking food, contrary to that of the Danube which is "good neither in food nor in drink, because it injures a person's intestines with its harshness." In contrast, the water of the Glan is "healthy and good for preparing food, drink, for bathing and for washing the face." One has the feeling here of a personal observation that was within her reach. Yet the comments that can be so explained are few in number, especially considering the amount and the quality of the knowledge accumulated in Hildegard's works.

We return to the title *Subtleties of Nature,* which well suits the quality of the knowledge proposed. One can indeed say that from the medical, alimentary, and environmental viewpoint, Hildegard helps us appreciate the unknown powers of what surrounds us: plants, animals, herbs, woods. Reading her unfolds unsuspected possibilities, secret powers, which have become very foreign to our world where everything is conditioned, packaged, chosen, and sorted beforehand. It is a world provided with a mysterious life, whose mysteries it invites us to examine. Certainly, chemists do this also, but only by giving us nothing of their research except the final point, the result. Hildegard invites us to renew our vision. Ecologists should be interested in her work. She seems to take us by the hand through the immense reserves of Nature to teach us to discern there what first escapes our senses. Hence the subtle value, in Hildegard's eyes, is the curative and beneficial value that plants, fruits, animals, fish, etc., can have for man. Each element of nature thus possesses its value, salutary or harmful, which the abbess's works teach us to discern.

Today's reader should certainly expect some surprises in approaching the different chapters of the *Physica* or of the *Liber Compositae Medicinae*. He or she should from the first get used to certain terms, those, for example, disconcerting to us, that allow a sort of summary classification in the temperament of plants as well as in human temperament. There is the quality—hot or cold, dry or moist—of each element, a basic classification that goes back to Aristotelian notions. Hildegard adds here a notion of her own invention that we have already had occasion to examine: "greenness" or "viridity," that life-power that rising sap manifests, which she invokes often in regard to plants, to be sure, but also in regard to all living creatures.

The modern reader is also continually struck by the absence of calculated amounts. We have the habit of counting and measuring by precise quantities. To be told to "cook vigorously some dittany in water. . . . [D]uring cooking, add two times of sempervivum and add some nettle, two times as much of sempervivum and stir it all in." Or else the amounts seem rather strange to us, as in this recipe: "Reduce to powder one part of ginger, a half-part of licorice and a third part made of zedoary and as much of ginger; weigh the resulting powder, take the same weight of sugar. All this should weigh more or less the weight of thirty pieces." Or again: "Take a measure of ginger and a little more of cinnamon, reduce to powder. Take some sage, a little less than of ginger, and some fennel, a little less than of sage, as well as some tansy, a little less than of sage; grind in a mortar, etc." Sometimes the quantity indicated consists of taking some "on the point of a knife"; or again, following a very widespread custom of the time, the measure is a half eggshell. In each case we are very far from the precision of our times. This is a point on which one cannot be demanding: the Middle Ages is a time when numbers are not very familiar, in complete contrast with ours, in which the use of the micron or the hundredth-of-a-second has become common.

Still, on many points the modern reader finds an affinity with the comments of Hildegard. Nowadays a certain sense of gentle medicine is beginning to spread; faced with the multitude of specialties that medical science—highly developed and certainly effective—presents, some people look for concern for the whole. Now the desire for balance that pervades all of Hildegard's work is striking. She is also attentive to the person, to his or her states of soul as well as to physical ailments. She hardly separates one from another.

In her works, for example, in those dealing with plants, we see the recurrence of her concern for healing "melancholy"; this is all the more fearful the more that it saps "greenness." Basically it arises from poorly eliminated black bile; it engenders bad humors from which come troubles in

metabolism and which lead to depression. It is also respon-
sible for attacks of gout and rheumatism as well as fits of
rage, all dreadful things. Thus there is a whole series of
prescriptions for eliminating this harmful black bile: good
meals, well-prepared, are of help, since human health is
maintained by a sound nutritious diet. Certain remedies
can act immediately, as does the rose in the case of irritability. "Take some rose and a little less of sage, reduce to
powder and at the moment when the irritability bursts out,
hold this powder near the nostrils. The sage indeed calms,
and the rose delights."

A whole series of remedies, and especially an appropriate
diet, enable the elimination of black bile. And this detailed
comment allows us to grasp what is essential in Hildegard's
process, her method as it were. She is not unaware of the ill
effects of black bile in the organism, which means that she
has absolutely correct views on the role of the liver and the
consequences of its possible disorders; immoderate irritability is one of these consequences. Now, one can calm this by
the sight of something beautiful that also gives off a sweet
odor—hence the rose, which will act even better if one adds
to it sage with its calming powers.

All this may seem a bit elementary, even simplistic.
However, we find in it a concern for taking care of the sick
person more than the sickness; an attention given to behav-
iors as effects of inner disorder; beauty and harmony as
necessary for human development—all principles that are
essential to Hildegard's thought. For her, the natural state

of a human is health, the lack thereof is destructive. Retrieving, maintaining, protecting a person's natural health, assuring the full use of his or her capabilities, is the business of daily vigilance over both spirit and body. Nature is an inexhaustible reserve of elements among which we must be able to discern, to be attentive to the "subtleties" that it conceals—consequently, to be attentive to diet, which enables one to preserve balance or to recover it if lost. This diet includes fasting—fasting that is not absolute, since it allows vegetable broths, fruit juices, and diverse herbal teas—that relaxes the organism and allows it to eliminate excesses periodically, thus to recover calm.

As for food, it should be suited to age and to general condition, modulated according to the individual and the season. Hildegard especially recommends three products that she declares are entirely beneficial and proper for developing in everybody that "greenness" which is for humans what sap is for plants. Her choice does not fail to surprise us somewhat. First of all there is spelt, a not-very-common cereal now; she assures us that it is the best. Wheat is useful for bread; especially in the form of "whole bread"—"it brings about good flesh and good blood"; for people in good health, she also recommends oats, while indicating that they are harmful to sick people. Finally, rye makes one "strong and vigorous." But there is nothing like spelt: analysis in our time proves that it contains all the vitamins necessary for balanced nutrition.

The chestnut is presented as "a fruit useful against every

weakness in a human." It is recommended to eat it often, whether in season or in the form of flour. There is a vegetable that also has very positive effects: it is fennel, which "makes a person jovial, assures fine color in the face, a good body odor and good digestion." As for fruits, the best for Hildegard is the apple, especially when "it has aged and the peel becomes wrinkled in winter." It is as good for the sick as it is for the healthy; everybody will benefit equally from eating it, cooked or grilled.

These are some products that are entirely positive, suitable for maintaining perfect health and good humor; for Hildegard is very attentive to "everything that pleases the human heart." For her it is necessary that foods be pleasing, that they be prepared in a pleasant manner; she always insists on the agreement between whatever nature provides that is harmonious and the benefit resulting from it for humans. "The perfume of the first bloom of lily and the perfume of their flowers delights the human heart and stirs good thoughts," she writes. She also advises lavender, which helps to give "pure knowledge and a pure spirit." She recommends drinking lavender in a decoction mixed with some wine or, if this is not possible, in honey water—such a drink, lukewarm, "allays the pains of the liver and the lungs."

The majority of plants to be used as remedies are prepared in decoction, generally with some wine—"preferably good wine." Hildegard also recommends poultices, applications of hot plants wrapped in a cloth and placed on the sick area, even on the head, since she is very attentive to brain fatigue. Or again, she recommends baking little flat-breads containing the indicated remedy: "When a person's brain is fatigued and, so to speak, empty, reduce wild thyme to powder, mix this powder with wheaten flour in some water, make little flatbreads with it, eat them often and the brain will feel better," she assures. She proposes a similar remedy based on nutmeg: "Take a nutmeg with an equal amount of cinnamon and a bit of clove; reduce to powder; with this powder, some wheaten flour, and a little water, make little flatbreads and eat them often; this prepa-ration sweetens the bitterness of the body and of the spir-it, opens the heart, sharpens dulled senses, gladdens the soul, purifies the senses, diminishes harmful humors, brings good sugar to the blood and fortifies it."

Hildegarde does not limit herself to minor difficulties or daily life; the same fennel in which she finds only positive virtues is recommended by her for women suffering in labor. "If a woman is suffering much during labor, have some perfumed herbs such as fennel and azarum cooked slowly and carefully in water; pour the water out, and place the herbs while still warm around her thighs and on her back; wrap them with cloth carefully so that the pain might vanish and that her womb might open more easily and less painfully." She recommends sempervivum for male sterility, and also, in plain terms, curly endive for calming "a man's amorous desire." "If a man's loins are too vigorous, he should have some curly endive cooked in water and, while bathing, place these cooked and warm leaves around his hips; let him repeat this often, and he will thus extinguish his desire without harming his health." For women having their period, she recommends drinking an infusion of chamomile.

To the deaf she advises the use of horehound: "Cook some horehound in water, remove it from the water, and let the vapor penetrate into the ears and place the warm horehound on the ears and the head, and hearing will improve." For eyesight, she advises eating dandelion, or else "in summer when they are green, often place leaves of fern on the eyes for sleeping; they purify the eyes and dissipate haze in vision." Fern possesses in addition all sorts of virtues that she does not fail to list. Concerning eyesight, the most advanced medicine of our time will not disagree with the following lines: "If water and blood lessen in the eyes of a human being, as a result of advanced age or of some sickness, he should go and walk," she writes, "in fields of green grass, and gaze at it for some time until his eyes moisten, as if they were shedding tears, because the greenery of the grass eliminates the trouble in the eyes and makes them pure and clear." It is known today that the eye adjusts out to thirty meters, and that this distance is not easily found in everyday city life, and that a stay in the country before a green field will help the eyes to rest and grow strong. She also recommends very pure water "that has not been used," and also, an old remedy of experience: "the drops that fall from vine stocks early in the morning up until midday . . . should be collected in the morning in a small vessel." The sap of young apple leaves also seems to her to be suitable for strengthening the eyes. "The eyelids should be moderately anointed, like dew falling on grass." Or else, "place them on the eyes over a compress cloth."

Perusing Hildegard's works, whether the *Simple Medicine* or the *Composite Medicine,* thus offers an immense variety of lessons of life of all sorts, to say nothing of the rediscovery of a poetic dimension of nature, if only through the names themselves (Guillaume Apollinaire thus called to mind "the anemone and the columbine"): One passes from the speedwell to the hawkweed to the birthwort; the names unfold like the millefleurs of fifteenth-century tapestries, such as origanum, potentilla, or agrimony. Upon reading her books, one perceives that nature in our times is probably to be rediscovered, and our modern ecologists should perhaps perfect their knowledge of it. It is pleasing to learn that while dill makes a human sad, the violet in contrast helps him to fight melancholy; that betony stimulates the spirit of consciousness and that eyesight improves with viewing at length a tuft of thyme; that fern is filled with beneficial powers that help in combatting sorcery of all kinds; that myrrh dissipates fantasies and that madder cures bouts of fever.

Yet it is no less interesting to note that, through the variety of this botany, that many of these products have disappeared, for lack of sufficient return, in a time when only the economic criterion prevails. Our cultures have been notably impoverished since the twelfth century. For example, Hildegard insists on the benefits of beans; in her time when the potato was unknown, they were the usual starchy food along with peas. "Beans are warm, good for eating by people in good health and in full strength; they are better than peas. . . . Bean flour is good and useful for the healthy person as for a sick one, for it is light and is easily digested." In contrast, peas, she says, while "good to eat for someone who is of a warm nature . . . nevertheless, since it is cold by nature, it does not help the sick, since during digestion it causes in them many discharges of humors." Now peas have remained common in our nutrition, while the bean has become rare.

One can also regret the disappearance of saffron, which was cultivated even in England, and is no longer found except in rare regions of Spain. The cultivation of hemp has been abandoned nearly everywhere—with the regrettable exception of *Cannabis indica,* from which hashish is derived. Nowadays, where forests disappear in order to furnish the huge quantities of paper consumed in the world, *Cannabis sativa,* the hemp of our fields, would furnish paper of excellent quality, and would be suitable for filling land that must be left fallow.

In reading Hildegard's medical works, we rediscover an unsuspected part of our environment, and it is no small surprise that it is restored to us by a mystic who could have contented herself with wonder as she discovered the universe.

CHAPTER VIII

JOURNEYS AND PREACHING

THROUGHOUT HER EXISTENCE, the surprising personality of Hildegard of Bingen is manifest. It is rare, it is indeed exceptional, that a nun, a religious having chosen the contemplative life, leaves her convent, without thereby abandoning her vocation. This vocation involves stability, part of the commitment made by the nun when she makes her profession of vows. Certain women religious, particularly abbesses, have had to make new foundations, which has caused them to leave their original convent; this would be the case of a Saint Teresa of Avila, for example. In the same manner, Hildegard herself had left, we have seen, the double community of Disibodenberg in order to found in 1150 the convent dedicated to Saint Rupert, close to Bingen. Again, in 1165, she founded the convent of Eibingen, on the other side of the Rhine; this last convent would bear her name, Saint Hildegard, up to our day.

Yet even more amazing are the journeys that she undertook for the purpose of preaching. The cloister for religious women in her time was certainly less severe and strict than it became thereafter, when the constitution *Periculoso* of Pope Boniface VIII at the end of the thirteenth century— in 1298 to be exact—limited them solely to a confined existence. This severity became accentuated as time went on: In the sixteenth and seventeenth centuries, women were allowed to found only totally cloistered orders. It is in a completely different context that the life of a religious woman unfolded in the twelfth century.

Still, for us at a distance, it is a strange sight to see an abbess who on four different occasions goes on the road in order to preach. It was even believed that she went to Paris and Tours, as the writer of one *Life* of hers states, but this is probably a mistake. One of those who recorded her revelations, Wibert de Gembloux, made the journey after Hildegard's death and showed her works to masters in the schools of Paris and Tours (we know that at the time the university of Paris did not yet exist); this is without doubt why the visionary's writings soon became known in France. John of Salisbury, the famous bishop of Chartres, speaks about her in a letter dated in 1167, and mentions the great trust in her that Pope Eugene III manifested. In the thirteenth century, Vincent of Beauvais could not fail to know about her, and he names her in his *Speculum historiale*. "At that same time," he writes,

in Germany there was an admirable virgin to whom the divine power had granted such graces that, although she was a layperson and unlettered [the term "layperson" is to be taken here in opposition to "cleric," designating those who frequented schools], nevertheless in a marvelous way she had learned, often being transported in dreaming, not only to express herself, but also to dictate in Latin, in such a way that through dictation she wrote books on the Catholic faith.

Now, it seems that it is possible, through close study of Hildegard's correspondence—which was gathered carefully and published in the Latin Patrology in the last century—to attempt to reconstitute the sermons that she delivered in certain places, or in any case to retrieve the subject of these sermons.

Besides the trip that she took to Ingelheim, it seems likely that the nun's first journey, for her first preaching, led her to Trier in 1160, probably around the time of Pentecost. Shortly after her passage, the city's prelates wrote to her, asking her to be so kind as to send them in writing what she had taught them in person. The request was sent to her by the provost of the church of Saint Peter, namely the cathedral, surrounded, he said, by all the clergy of Trier. He worded this request in terms full of respect, even affection.

"Since by divine permission the thoughts of many hearts have been revealed to you," he writes, citing Saint Luke,

by the divine will we love you with all the impetus of our body and all the devotion of our spirit. We indeed know that the Holy Spirit dwells in you and that through him many things have been shown to you that are unknown to other people. For since you left our midst, after you had come here, shortly afterward, on the day of Pentecost, through a higher disposition whereby you had foretold to us that a menace from God was imminent for us, we have seen and experienced around us and among us many hardships of Churches and many dangers on people's part, for we had neglected, as your enlightened judgment revealed to us, to appease the wrath of God, and if his vengeance had not been withdrawn thanks to God's mercy, perhaps we would have succumbed to despair under the weight of these same dangers. And since God is in you, and his very words issue from your mouth, we implore your deeply maternal love so that you might set down for us what you have said to us in person. . . . May God's protection remain always over you and that what he has begun in you he might bring to a good end.

One can fairly pose the question of material means, we could say techniques, that Hildegard used for traveling from Bingen to Trier. It does not seem impossible that she would use in part the river route, tracing the course of the Nahe perhaps as far as the region where the river is narrowly confined between two high banks—at the confluence of the Idar, on the heights of Oberstein—to take thereafter the route heading west and reach the old Roman city. Whatever the comforts of river transport, the course of the Moselle is indeed extremely sinuous in its last stretch between the Rhine and Trier; in contrast Hildegard seems to know the Nahe well, which she describes, as we have said, in her work *Physica*.

The city of Trier had an obvious place in the visionary's

life. That is where the famous synod of 1147–1148 took place; it gave her in some way the right to be, or to become, what she was. The city's extraordinarily rich past further inspired her. We have already mentioned that Trier had been, at the gates of the "barbarian realms," the Roman encampment par excellence, the staging place for the armies assigned to watch the borders of the vast Empire. The *Porta Nigra* still attests this Roman presence. It was at the time of its construction, at the end of the second century, the northern gate of the fortifications that surrounded the city over a length of more than six kilometers. In the eleventh century a hermit, Saint Simeon, originally from Syracuse, settled in the gate, or rather in its ruins; after his death the bishop of Trier, Poppo of Babenberg, dedicated to him the church that he built in the western tower. A cloister laid out in the neighborhood was available to monks grouped in the quarters of this same tower—which perhaps constituted, it is thought, the oldest monastery in Germany.

Hildegard probably saw this cloister of Saint Simeon, but she was especially interested, judging from her poetic output, in the abbey church of Saint Maximin. This very old Benedictine abbey—dating from the Carolingian epoch—was the largest and the richest of the archdiocese of Trier. It was utterly destroyed by French troops under orders of Louis XIV in 1674. Only in 1987 did excavations uncover a large fourth-century church rising amid graves (south of the current Church of Saint Paulinus).

This is the place to recall the quite surprising musical talent with which Hildegard was endowed, shown by her more than seventy compositions, now recovered and available thanks to the labors of Dr. Christopher Page. The sequence of Saint Maximin has even been the object of a cassette tape published under his direction.[7] He has brought out perfectly the value of Hildegard's musical accomplishments, which are well within the line of plain chant: meditative music that keeps tranquil control within ecstasy and leads the person singing to a development of interior life much more than to new, surprising, or chance musical effects. Evidence of this is the sequence that begins *Columba aspexit* ("The dove saw through the slits of the shutter. . . ").

In this, one finds images familiar to Hildegard, those that come freely from her pen both during her visions and in her correspondence: "This lofty tower, made of the wood of Lebanon and of cypress, is adorned with hyacinths and diamonds, a city that dominates the arts of all other artisans." And she continues to evoke through images those who carry out the sacred liturgy in the abbey: "O you who prepare the balm, you who are in the very sweet greenness of the king's gardens, you ascend to the heights when you perform the holy Sacrifice in the midst of rams." The verse cannot be understood unless one knows

[7] Hyperion KA 66 039.

that, in the Apocalypse, balm and perfumes in general symbolize the prayers of the saints, and that the rams evoke those of Exodus when they are sacrificed in the course of the ordination of the sons of Aaron. Undoubtedly Hildegard by this image is designating priests, even the young monks surrounding the celebrant at the altar of Saint Maximin. The music is indispensable here for appreciating the beauty of this sequence, but the images that are comprised in it reflect perfectly Hildegard's language. It is obviously not known at what date this superb sequence dedicated to Saint Maximin was composed by the visionary, but it attests in any case the depth of the impression she gained in Trier in the abbey dedicated to the saint.

The abbey of Saint Matthias still exists in our times. It is also, along with the cathedral, the sole example of Romanesque art that Trier still possesses, and it is closely tied to the history of the city, since it was consecrated by Pope Eugene III when he came to hold the famous synod in 1147. Earlier it was dedicated to Saint Eucharius, the city's first bishop, and it was precisely during its construction that the old altar was discovered containing the relics of Saint Matthias—the apostle who had been chosen to replace Judas after his betrayal. This discovery made the abbey church a place of pilgrimage much-frequented since the era of Hildegard.

Still, without doubt it was in the cathedral that the nun preached: the magnificent *Dom,* the oldest church in Germany, which the horrors of our twentieth-century wars fortunately spared. It was built by Constantine himself, and today still preserves a certain number of mementos in its treasury that tradition connects to Saint Helen, the emperor's mother. Sacked a first time by the Franks in the fifth century, it suffered the same treatment by the Normans in 882. It was rebuilt by Bishop Poppo of Babenberg at the beginning of the eleventh century, and the following centuries added notably the ribbed vaults that now cover the nave, while precious relics were gathered there: among these are the Holy Tunic, exposed in our time in a special chapel; the manuscripts produced by the famous *scriptorium,* and various treasures (of which some have since been kept in the diocesan museum or in the city museum), as well as the Market Cross erected at the time of the city's restoration after the destruction caused by the Normans. All of this makes Trier an exceptional jewel of history and art—and it was there that in 1908 the first measures were taken by decree for the preservation and restoration of historical monuments—measures fortunately imitated in the majority of Western countries since then.

The city offers, as well, the oldest example of those magnificent German cathedrals with a double apse, choir on one side, the other side on the west. Its beauty is imposing, whatever the importance of restorations and additions made over the course of time, especially after a fire such as that of 1137. (It had consumed the new church undertaken by the famous bishop Willigis, after an earlier fire had burned the structure on the very day of its consecration,

August 30, 1009.) These two apses where the choirs respond to one another, filling the vast edifice, symbolize both the architectural splendors and the prodigious musical sense of the epoch, of which Hildegard herself is a living example.

Thus it was in a setting extraordinarily rich with historical remembrances, and quite worthy of a personage like herself, that the abbess probably delivered her first sermon in public.

First, in a few words she drew her self-portrait. "I am a poor little figure, and in myself I have neither health, nor power, nor courage, nor knowledge." Yet this is what she said that she had heard from the "mystical light of a true vision"; and the following has a solemn tone:

> The doctors and the masters refuse to sound the trumpet of justice; this is why the Orient of good works is extinguished in them, he who illumines the whole world and who is as the mirror of light. The Orient indeed should shine in them with knowledge and rule their various precepts, just as the sphere of the sun is diverse. The Auster (the South) of virtues, with its warmth, is among them cold as winter, for they do not have in themselves the good works burning with the fire of the Holy Spirit, since they are dry and lack greenness. The Occident of mercy is also turned into blackness of ashes, for they do not apply to themselves the Passion of Christ nor do they meditate on it vividly as they should—he who out of humility has come down into our humanity and there buried his divinity, just as

it happens that the sun conceals itself from one time to another. But the North, with the wind of Aquilo, breathes on them since each of them transforms the extension [of his own will] for the punishment of men, somewhat like a hairshirt enveloping a person's body.

Then they fail to show themselves through good works to the Orient, nor do they shine with the ardor of the sun, nor do they withdraw from evil toward the Occident, but with Aquilo of the North they conceal themselves in their hearts' own will. Because of this, the devil sends three black winds of Aquilo with a glad hiss. The first goes with pride and hate against the Orient who is extinguished. The second goes against the South, by forgetting God. The third goes against the Occident by faithlessness.

An explanation of the Old Testament follows through its main figures, presented as Hildegard loves to do it. This is to say that one can recognize fully her own manner, including in this preamble which speaks of the forces of the universe: the cardinal points, the winds, all the cosmic energies, the evocation of which has as large a part in her work, as in what follows, the explanation of the Redemption, which probably would have constituted the framework of her sermon given in Trier, of which the clergy desired a written record.

The general theme of it is God's indefatigable kindness, which constantly calls man to his presence, combats his inertia, and reanimates his always flagging zeal.

unworthy as I am. So I humbly ask you that, as divine mercy allows you, you ask God what I must do, and that you kindly tell me your counsel through the bearer of these present letters; what must I do and how to do it, so that the name of Christianity be exalted in my time, and so that the harsh fierceness of the Saracens might be repelled, and whether it should be useful for me that I stay in this land or that I return to it. Perhaps you may know about this as far as it concerns me, and you may know it through divine revelation or will be able to know it.

Greetings in Christ, dear sister, and know that I greatly wish to hear your advice and that I have the greatest confidence in your prayers.

Hildegard's answer adopts a solemn tone:

O son of God—for he himself has fashioned you in the first man—hear the words that I have seen and heard in my soul and spirit, and the watchful body, when, in order to answer your question I turned toward the true light.

In a few words she recalls for him the just judgment by which Adam was expelled from Paradise, how those who had forgotten God were buried by the flood and how the gentlest Lamb, the Son of God, hanging on a cross, saved humans by blotting out all their crimes and their sins. These are general considerations appropriate for making Count Philip reflect, for he had a reputation as a quick-

Adam indeed, because he broke the precepts of God, lost the vision of heavenly things and his garment of light, and was sent to a place of misery. The zeal of the Lord then drove out Cain, for having shed the blood of his brother whom he had killed. Many were the peoples who appeared among the children of Adam, who had forgotten God, to the point that they did not want to acknowledge themselves as human, but, sinning in a shameful manner, lived like cattle. The exceptions were the children of God who separated themselves from these men and from their loves, and among these Noah was born. Then the zeal of God showed itself, and the Spirit of the Lord was borne over the waters and opened the clouds, and he released the waters in a flood. Thus the earth was washed of criminal faults and of the blood of Abel which it had drunk. It was God who did this.

A second phase starts with the figure of Abraham:

The Holy Trinity showed a great work in Abraham, designating him in advance and teaching him obedience so that he might leave his country and . . . in Abraham's obedience, God changed the fault of Adam, and in his circumcision he signified death, and gave to see in advance in the fruitfulness of a sterile woman that another woman would engender another son, since the Son of God accomplished everything that had been foretold beforehand in his Nativity.

Thereafter came Moses the lawgiver and, from time to time, those who awakened the spirit of repentance in the midst of evil actions by men, as did Jonas. And Hildegard continues:

> After God had prefigured what he willed to do, he remembered what he had said, that he would crush the head of the serpent. And he made a woman, the Virgin, in obedience and chastity, and he filled her with every good, so that the pride that was in Eve was consumed in her. And this Virgin conceived the Son of God by the Holy Spirit . . . . God then completed this work which he had thus prepared in the flesh, and he gave to this Son who was his all fleshly things in order to render them spiritual, for he is the flesh of holiness who proceeds from another nature, which the serpent's counsel never violated. Therefore it came about that the same Son of God renewed the old Law in the water of baptism; by faith and obedience, and by abstinence from carnal desires, he showed the way of holiness.

And she concludes this tableau of the passage from the old to the new Covenant:

> Then the Orient shone with his power and the South burned with its heat and the Occident was no longer harmful nor the North buffeted by Aquilo, since by the Passion of Christ they were tempered, until the coming of a tyrant beginning with whom every evil, injustice and betrayal showed themselves.

Hildegard continues by noting that the Law in her time is neglected among the people of the spirituals—the clerics—

who forget to do and to teach the good. "The masters and the prelates sleep without troubling themselves any more about justice." She warns that the temporal powers will not take long to come and destroy cities and cloisters and that those who let themselves go "with woman's weaknesses" will soon be punished for it. She urges those who stay away from evil, as did Elijah, Noah, and Lot in their times, to reveal themselves and purify themselves. Thanks to them and to other wise seculars, people will become good again and will live in a holy manner and then "powers, courage and holiness will return to the people." She ends by saying that she has seen Trier animated by a new fire, the one that appeared over the disciples in tongues of fire, and therefore it was all adorned, so that its streets were illumined with miracles in a golden faith "while at this time it is surrounded by folly and by bad customs and afflicted with all sorts of evils . . . which cannot be brought to an end unless they are wiped out by repentance, as was the case in the time of Jonah" (letter 49).

It seems likely that after her sojourn in Trier, Hildegard went to Metz, which is expressly mentioned in her *Life* as having been visited by her. It is therefore probable that she gave a sermon in the cathedral there as well; not the resplendent Gothic cathedral that can be seen today, entirely rebuilt in the following century, but the one of which the Romanesque crypt survives; she probably walked on the floor of this crypt. After Trier, the city was easy to reach by following the course of the Moselle. In that period Metz was an important city, commercially and culturally. Its *scriptorium* was famous and has left us considerable treasures, such as the *Sacramentaire de Drogon*, produced probably around 842. Hildegard certainly saw the church Saint-Pierre de la Citadelle, which still exists today, and admired in the treasury of the cathedral certain pieces that were later scattered, such as the famous cut crystal, dating from the era of Charles the Bald, representing the biblical story of Susanna (now it is in the British Museum). Nevertheless, we have no information concerning her preaching; no letter in her correspondence mentions it.

We find Hildegard again on the road, or rather along the rivers, probably around the year 1163. This was the period when she began her last work, *The Book of Divine Works;* it was for her also a time of long journeys and important preaching, the content of which is still striking for us today. It seems that for this second journey the Rhine was marked as the whole route. Hildegard indeed headed for Cologne; she probably stopped in Boppard, not far from Bingen; perhaps she then made a stop in Andernach, still on the Rhine. It is in that place, let us recall, that a knight lying very sick in bed believed he saw a vision in which the nun appeared to him saying: "In the name of him who said: 'You will lay your hands on the sick and they will get better,' let this illness leave you, and be healed." The young knight then got up from his bed and, to everyone's wonderment, found himself cured.

The invitation made to Hildegard came from Philip, who said he was dean of the "Great Church," namely the cathedral of Cologne, in his name and in that of all the clergy of the city. The research by Sabina Flanagan allows the dating of this letter, for the same Philip became provost in 1165, and he would later become archbishop of the diocese of Cologne. As the Trier clergy did earlier, he reminds Hildegard that she kindly chose to stop among them, and he asks her to send them in writing what she had spoken to them in person.

Since we love your maternal piety, we make known to you that, after you left us, since by divine order you had come to us where you opened to us the words of life, as God inspired you, we have been led to the greatest admiration for what God has worked in so frail a vessel and in so frail a sex of humanity, for so many wonders of his secrets that he inspired. But the Spirit blows where he wills [he adds, quoting Saint John], for by many signs it is evident that he has chosen a place pleasing to him in you, in the depths of your heart. [And he continues, after having recommended to Hildegard's prayers the people around him:] We ask you, then, that you might entrust to letters what you earlier said to us in person, and that you send them to us, for, given over as we are to carnal desires, we easily forget by negligence the spiritual things that we neither see nor hear.

In response, Hildegard begins by presenting a vision familiar to her: a prodigious tableau of the universe, into

which are inserted the main figures of the Bible, once
again.

> He who was and who is and who will come [she begins, quot-
> ing the Apocalypse], says to the shepherds of the Church: he
> who was had to become a creature so that he would have in
> himself the testimony of testimonies, he who does all things as
> he wills them. . . . He who must come will purify all things and
> will renew them through other difficulties and will smooth the
> rough places in the times of the times, and will make every-
> thing new at once, and after purification will show the
> unknown things.
>
> A wind blew from him, saying: I have set the firmament
> with everything that adorns it, with no power lacking to it.
> Indeed it has eyes for seeing, ears for hearing, nostrils for
> smelling, a mouth for tasting. Indeed, the sun is like the light of
> its eyes, the wind like the hearing of its ears, the air its odor, the
> dew its taste, causing greenness to issue as is from the mouth.
> The moon as well gives the times of the times (the seasons and
> their unfolding) and thus unfolds the knowledge to humans.
> The stars, as if they were endowed with reason, are indeed so,
> for they go in a circle, and thus their rationality understands
> many things. And I have set four corners to the globe, of fire,
> of cloud and of water, and so I have joined, as by seams, all the
> extremities of the earth. I have filled the rocks with fire and
> water like bones, and I have inserted into the soil humidity and
> greenness like marrow. I have widened the abysses as those that
> support bodies by setting them, around which are the waters

that flow to maintain them. Thus, all things are constituted so that they will not vanish. If the clouds had neither water nor fire, they would be like ashes. But if the other luminaries did not get their light from the sun's fire, they would not shine through the waters, but would be blind.

After this evocation of the interdependence of all the elements of the universe, "instruments of man's edification that he understands by touching, kissing and embracing," Hildegard addresses the shepherds, as always in the name of the divine Light:

I have set you as the sun and the other luminaries so that you might shine for humans, by the fire of doctrine, brilliant with good fame, and that you might prepare ardent hearts. Thus did I in the first age of the world. I chose Abel, I loved Noah, I showed myself to Abraham, I chose Moses for the institution of the Law and I constituted the prophets as my beloved friends.

And she compares Abel to the moon, Noah to the sun, Abraham to the planets, Moses to the stars, and the prophets to the four cardinal points, which support the limits of the earth.

Yet she reproaches her listeners for their inertia.

Your tongues are mute in the voice that resounds from the trumpet of God, you who do not love holy rationality that holds like the stars the circle of circular revolution. The trum-

pet of God, this is the justice of God, which you should pon-
der with great care, by repeating it in the established rule and
in obedience, with holy discretion, by presenting it to the peoples at appropriate times, and not by commanding them
excessively. Yet, because of the stubbornness of your own will,
you do not do this. Thus your tongues lack the luminaries in
the firmament of God's justice, as when the stars do not shine.

And she rebukes them for acting like "bare snakes in
their caves" or for "dallying in the fantasies of childhood."
Finally, she exclaims as if on her own:

> Oh! what wickedness and enmity in that man does not wish
> to be turned toward the good neither for God nor for man,
> but that he seeks honor without work and eternal rewards
> without abstinence! . . . You have no eyes, for your works do
> not shine before people with the fire of the Holy Spirit, and
> you do not appeal to them by good example; thus the firma-
> ment of God's justice lacks in you the light of the sun, and the
> air lacks sweet odors in the edifice of virtues.

A long series of reproaches follows, in the first place of
laxity, of lack of zeal, of culpable weakness: "You should
be pillars of fire." She takes it further:

> Yes, thanks to the capacity for reason that God has given you,
> you reprimanded in all truth those who are subject to you, and
> they would not dare resist the truth. But as far as they could,

they would say that your word is true. . . . Therefore all wisdom that you have sought everywhere in the Scriptures and in study becomes devoured in the pit of your own will. It is as if you buried what you knew by having touched and experienced it, in order to fulfill your desires and to fatten your flesh like a small child who, in his infancy, does not know what he is doing.

She then takes as examples the obedience of biblical figures, their desire to hear and to put into practice the word that God spoke to them, summarizing it all in a forceful phrase: "You should be day, but you are night; for you will be either night or day; choose then on which side you want to stand." Then she develops examples through Scripture, up to the point where she comes to baptism, in which "the serpent was suffocated by confusion and death was destroyed and wounded; therefore the Church will beget a new generation through another way, for Eve was sterile of one life, and Mary brought a grace greater than Eve's harm."

Vigorous words, even vehement, which one imagines must have caused some shivers in the crowd—not just of the people, but especially of the clerics. This is an occasion for us to note that we are far from ecclesiastical unctuousness, which would reign in the classical era, among others, when Hildegard would have been condemned without recourse, for lack of respect toward prelates and hierarchy. Here we are faced with a very different mentality, and the liveliness of the language is accepted as a call to conversion, addressed to everyone, but especially to those who have chosen to transmit and make understood the word of God.

> Again I heard, from the living light, a voice saying: "O daughter of Zion, the crown of honor will tilt on the head of your children, and the mantle of the fullness of your riches will be threatened, for they will not have known the time that I have given them to see and to teach those subject to them. They have been given breasts to nourish their little children, which they do not offer to them as needed and when wanted, so that, as if lost, many of my children die of hunger, for their strength has not been restored by sound doctrine. They have one voice and they do not cry out. My works are also offered to them but are not carried out. They wish to have glory without merit and merit without work. This enables the Enemy to offer them his own goods, filling their eyes, ears and bellies with vices."

This vehemence of expression is motivated by the struggle that Hildegard wants to undertake.

She denounces some errors that are even worse than those of the people who err, "the customs of a scorpion, the works of a serpent"; showing that these errors could enter a previously healthy body, she hurls dreadful condemnations against the Cathars, whom she describes very astutely.

> Some people will come, seduced and sent by the devil, with a pale face and assuming an attitude of holiness, and they will

attach themselves to major secular leaders to talk to them about you: "Why do you keep these people near you, and why do you allow them into your circle, since they are poisoning the whole earth with their filthy iniquities? They are drunken and lustful people, and if you do not keep them away from you, the whole Church will be ruined."

The people who will say that about you [let us remember that she was addressing prelates and clergy] wear shabby capes of faded colors; they will come forward with close-cropped hair and will display themselves to everyone as having tranquil and serene customs. They do not like avarice, they have no money and practice in private such abstinence that it would be difficult to find anything in them to blame. Now, the devil is with these people: concealing his radiance, he shows himself to them as he was at the creation of the world before the fall, and sometimes becomes similar to the prophets and says: "The people speak in jest, saying that I show myself to them in the form of raging and unclean animals, and as flies. But now I want to fly on wings of wind in flashing lightning and penetrate them in such a way that they fulfill my every wish. This is why among humans I will make my exterior similar to almighty God." For it is the devil who does this through invisible spirits who, because of the evil works of humans, run among them in all directions, on gusts of winds and of air, innumerable as flies and mosquitoes that infest humans in swarms in the intensity of heat. He himself has indeed entered into these people in such a way that he does not take away their chastity. He allows them to be chaste because it is their wish to keep chastity.

And he continues, saying to himself, "God loves chastity and continence, which I will imitate in them." And so the ancient Enemy penetrates these people with demons in the air, in such a way that they refrain from shameful sins. Alas! Therefore other people who are there do not know what to do; they are like those who went before us in the early times. For the others, those who err in the Catholic faith, will respect these people and will serve them with all devotion, and will imitate them as much as possible. And the former will rejoice in their conversation, because they will seem to them to be among the just.

Thus, in her sermon delivered in Cologne about 1163 or 1164, Hildegard denounced a new form of heresy in which it is not hard to recognize the Cathars. To be sure, it was less a matter of a heresy properly speaking as of some kind of new religion, similar to the sects that we see in our twentieth century, and which, placing itself outside of Revelation, presupposed an initial dualism: two gods at the origin of creation, the one the creator of the visible, material, corporal world, and this was an evil god; the other, the creator of souls, of spirit, a good god, the only one that man should cleave to. A dozen years earlier, this "heresy" showed up in Languedoc; their adepts were called "Henricians," since there was a certain monk Henry who had been at the origin of their straying. This became quite widespread, especially around the county of Toulouse, and moved Saint Bernard himself to make a preaching tour there, shortly before his death. Once back in Clairvaux, he had written to the inhabitants of the city to urge them to persevere in right doctrine after his mission, which had been a success.

> Our sojourn in your midst [he wrote] was of short duration, but not without its fruits. The truth that has been manifested by us, not only by words, but also by acts [he was alluding to his miracles] has unmasked those wolves who, coming among you in sheepskins, devoured your people like a piece of bread. It has unmasked those foxes that were ravaging your vine, the very precious vine of the Lord; however, while they have been unmasked, they have not been caught. [He recommends mistrust toward those preachers of a new sort] who, wearing the appearance of piety, and rejecting virtue entirely, mix heavenly words with profane novelties of meaning or expression, as if mixing poison with honey. Beware of them as poisoners and recognize them as rapacious wolves under their sheepskins.

This was also Hildegard's warning; the description that she gave of these people dressed in old worn and faded rags, with pale faces and shorn heads, who have all the appearances of continence and chastity and "who do not love women, but shun them," makes them easily recognizable.

In fact, the Cathars would not take long to pullulate in Rhenish lands, a very commercial region and prospering fully in the period when Hildegard was preaching; and it seems that this development of commerce and urban life where profit became the dominant concern had fertile ground for a tainted doctrine of spirituality, yet alien to the Gospel and drawing its source from ancient Manichaean affirmations. A kind of dualism, utterly simplistic, which identified evil with the body itself and consequently dreaded women, through whom life is transmitted and who by procreation accomplish the work of the "evil god." A logic without nuance, that reduces body and matter to being instruments of sin, which does nothing but foster the eternal and troubling distinction between good and evil, the very object of Adam's temptation: to decide for oneself what is one's good and what is one's evil.

The nun displayed, in describing the near future, some surprising gifts of prophecy. She first did this in denouncing the Manichaean maneuvers:

When these beings have confirmed the development of their error in this fashion [about which she spoke], doctors and sages who faithfully persevere in the Catholic faith will pursue them [the Manichaeans] and persecute them everywhere; but not all, for some among them are very courageous soldiers in God's justice. Likewise, they will be unable to disturb congregations of saints whose conversation is holy. This is why they give advice to princes and to rich people so that they might compel the masters of the Church and other spiritual people who are their subjects, under blows from sticks and rods, until they become just. This will be done by some, whereby others will be terrified and afraid. Nevertheless, according to what Elijah says, "the multitude of the just will be saved, and they ought not to be confounded in these errors nor be destroyed in their foundations."

Nonetheless these seducers [the Cathars], at the beginning of the seduction of their error, say to women: "It is not permitted for you to be with us, but since you do not have enlightened teachers, obey us, do everything that we tell and order you to do, and you will be saved." And in this way they attract women to them and lead them to share in their error. After this, with their spirit all swelled with pride, they will say: "We have controlled them all." Thereafter, however, they will join with these same women to commit lust in secret, and thus their iniquity and that of their sect will be uncovered.

In the course of her sermon, the nun seems more and more inspired. She foretells a dreadful end for the adherents of the sect:

But God has prepared for your evil works, which are without light, a vengeance in which he will leave you helpless, for he will not call for equity for you, but will declare you iniquitous. . . . You are a bad example of the spirit of humans, since a stream of good renown does not flow from you. As a result, you will have neither food to feed you, nor clothing to cover you in fitting consideration of the soul, but of unjust works without the good of knowledge. This is why your honor will perish and the crown will fall from your head. . . . For it must be that, through tribulation and contrition, the perverse works of humans must be liquidated. Nonetheless, many trials will befall those who bring about afflictions on others by their impiety. Indeed, these faithless people, seduced by the devil, will be so many brooms to punish you, for you do not honor God purely, and they are going to torment you until your iniquities have been driven out.

And she foresees, against these perverse seducers, some dreadful chastisements:

Princes and other grand personages are going to turn against them and will kill them like enraged wolves, everywhere that they find them.

She continues further, and her prophecy then takes a turn that surprises us, by foretelling a dawn of justice that

will then rise among spiritual people and which, at first, will begin with a small number, and they will not want to have much power nor much wealth, things that kill the soul, but they will say: "Have mercy on us, for we have sinned." These, indeed, will be comforted and will come into justice outside of past suffering and fear, just as the angels were comforted in the love of God when the devil fell. And so, as a consequence, they will live in humility and will not wish to rebel against God by performing evil works. Yet, freed from all kinds of errors, from then on they will persevere with a very courageous power of righteousness. As a result, many people will be astounded that such a violent storm was the forerunner of this gentleness. People who will have lived before that time will have undergone many violent struggles against their own will, at the peril of their bodies from which they were unable to free themselves. However, in your time, you will have many troubles and struggles against your own wills and your poorly restrained behavior, in which you will have to suffer all sorts of tribulations.

One can wonder if the nun is not announcing here, after the punishments to which the Cathars exposed themselves, the dawning of gentleness that the new orders would represent at the beginning of the thirteenth century, the Friars Minor at the call of Saint Francis, and the Friars Preachers at the call of Saint Dominic, who would have as distinctive traits gentleness, humility, and penance, instituting a new page of the Gospel, a new flowering of the reign of God's love. In other words, it seems that one can interpret this passage of Hildegard's preaching as foreknowledge of that unexpected regeneration that the mendicant orders would bring about—and at first precisely in the regions of Languedoc where the heresy raged with the greatest violence, both in its manifestations and in its repression.

To summarize these events briefly, it should be noted that one of the reasons for the Cathars' success was the poverty that they displayed—at least the "perfect" did, those who had received the *consolamentum*, and who committed themselves to all the austerities by rule, since this was a two-tier religion, and the simple adepts did not receive this *consolamentum* until the moment of their death. It is certain that the clergy of that time, especially in the rich Rhenish regions, as also in the region of Toulouse, had difficulty in mastering their wealth; this temptation is always present, in every case always cropping up again, especially in periods of prosperity. Hildegard was not the last to scold clerics for their laxity and their tendencies toward ease. Even the rigorous orders such as the Cistercians did not take long to succumb to it. The abbot of Cîteaux, in the thirteenth century, would use a carriage for his travels, the luxuriousness of which would have attracted the wrath of Saint Bernard.

The spread of sects everywhere coincided with the increase of wealth and the development of urban life; Catharism thus spread at first in the Rhine Valley, before showing itself especially in the region of Toulouse. The count of Toulouse, Raymond V, called the bishops' attention to the sect's expansion, while his son Raymond VI favored it, up to the point when he was accused in 1208 of ordering the assassination of the papal legate Pierre de Castelnau, who had come to issue reprimands. This murder in the *Midi* around Toulouse unleashed what later would be called the Albigensian War, with excesses and horrors that are known; all this led to the institution of the tribunals of the Inquisition in 1231.

However, in the meantime one Dominic de Guzman, traveling through the region of Toulouse and noticing the progress of the Catharist sects, had reacted with an appeal to evangelical poverty, as well as to better knowledge of correct doctrine, excluding all dualism. Very significantly, he first created in 1206 a monastery of women, bringing together converts from Catharism; he then established the first mendicant order, that of the Friars Preachers. Soon one Francis of Assisi, for his part, created a double branch, male and female, of mendicants—Franciscans and Poor Clares. The latter, with Saint Clare at their head, obtained from pontifical authority the "privilege of poverty," by which they prevented themselves from accepting any "benefice," land or property, beyond the ground on which they lived. A new form of contemplative life was thus born, at the beginning of the thirteenth century, destined to spread throughout the West and to bring even to the East, near and far, the call of the Gospel.

The remainder of Hildegard's sermon delivered in Cologne grappled with the dualist error.

> God indeed saw in advance his work in Adam, whose flesh and bone he made from mud, when he breathed into him the breath of life. And when the Spirit leaves a human, flesh and bones fall into ashes, but they will be renewed on the last day. That God has made man from slime prefigures the Old Law which he would give to man. But that this same man would stand on the ground, in flesh and blood, shows the spiritual Law that the Son of God has brought about by himself. . . . There he finds himself truly renewed. . . . You, God who have

created everything, will send your Spirit at the sound of the last trumpet, and humans will rise into immortality. In this way they will have reason neither to grow nor to waste away, nor will they be turned into dust. And so you will renew the face of the earth, knowing well that body and soul will be in a single consciousness and a single perfection. This is what God will do, in whom there is no beginning and no end. For God has nothing to look back upon, since he himself is everything. And he himself created man, in whom he placed his work and his miracles and to whom he entrusted the whole edifice of virtue by which they tend toward him, toward what God himself loves, he who is Charity.

[The sermon ends on a pressing entreaty:] At present, O children of God, listen and understand what the Spirit of God says to you, lest you perish for the most part. The Spirit of God says to you: "Look in your city and your region, and reject far from you those wicked people who are worse than Jews and similar to Sadducees. For, as long as they dwell among you, you cannot be safe." The Church laments and deplores the iniquity of these people, for they contaminate her children with their iniquity. This is why you must reject them far from you lest your assembly and your city perish, since, in Cologne, the festivities of the royal wedding have been prepared and they resound in your public places. For me, a shy and poor old woman, I have wearied myself greatly these past two years in presenting all this before the masters and doctors and other sages, everywhere that they live, in person; but, since the Church was divided, I had to still this voice for the time being.

Hildegard would have the chance to return to this subject, the importance of which she had evidently grasped, and to repeat energetically her warnings, in the letter that she addressed to the prelates of Mainz (letter 47), and later in a sermon she delivered during her third journey. There she expresses even more explicitly in what the error of the Manichaeans consists, and against their doctrine she rehabilitates the human body, while demonstrating the close union of body and spirit.

> Happy indeed is the human whom God has conceived as a tabernacle of wisdom with the sensuality of his five senses. Until the end of his life, thanks to the holy desires for good works and with his hunger for justice and the sweetest virtues which can never tire him, he ascends continually from newness to newness, by the grace of God. And so he comes to the glory of unchanging life that lasts without one growing tired of it, and always without end. Therefore God, until the last days, makes all things new, all things that are in his knowledge alone and that, until the last days, he has willed to do with might and according to his power. . . . Body and soul are one with their particular powers and their name, as are flesh and blood; and by these three, namely by body and soul and by rationality, a human is completed and produces works.

From this double nature that is man, both body and spirit, she moves on to the birth of the Word, who is also incarnate:

The Word, who in the beginning was in God, was made flesh of the Virgin Mary, the living source who refreshes with living waters those who believe in him; as he said, "Streams of living water will flow from the bosom of the one who believes in me," [she says, quoting Saint John. And she continues by showing that] the Son of man himself eats and drinks as he has allowed man to do, so that his flesh and his blood might grow and be fed, lest they lack anything for carrying out their duty and lest they waste away. But the serpent poisoned this food when the first humans were expelled from Paradise, whereby, and at the suggestion of the devil, they begot in pain their children whom they had conceived in sin. But the Son of God made this deadly concept of man vanish, when he was conceived and born by the Holy Spirit of the Virgin Mary, without any sin of manly nature. Then the Son of God gave his body and his blood under the form of bread and wine to his disciples; for these are the two things that are suitable and can be prepared for him. Just as the grain is hidden in the soil and, without any other mingling except by the warmth of the sun and the moisture of the water, is born by the grace of God, in a hidden manner, in its greenness, so also grapes, not by a mingling but by the mystical grace of God, sprout and grow. Thus the Son of God, without any mingling, becomes true man in his hidden divinity.

From the Incarnation Hildegard then moves on to the Eucharist.

For God himself, who signifies both fire and water, is at this point hidden in immense depth, which utterly surpasses the power of intellect of the human spirit; therefore he indeed removed in the Virgin Mary all carnal desire, so that his Son put on humanity from her without any fire of sin. The Holy Spirit, who is the living source, came over her like a very gentle humor, descending like dew on grain.

This same power of the Most High that came over Mary, realizing in her the flesh and the blood of the Son of God, descends on the offering of bread and wine, from the open wounds of Jesus Christ, so that this same offering of bread and wine, in a hidden manner, in the presence of God and of the holy angels, becomes transformed into flesh and blood—indeed just as the wheat and the wine, by their hidden greenness, which humans cannot see, begin to sprout. But since man, after having washed away his guilt by the pouring of baptism, very often falls into sin, the wounds of the same Son of God remain open for as long as man, filled with reason, will sin, so that through penance and confession he is washed in his wounds and is accepted.

But these people known as heretics and Sadducees deny the most holy humanity of the Son of God and the holiness of his body and of his blood which is presented in the offering of bread and wine. This is why the devil, who took his origin from him who has no beginning nor end, and who at the start of his elevation contradicted the unity of the Eternal Divinity, scatters a dust of death over the whole world through the medium of these people. He is indeed a liar, because he imbues the eyes of these people with the blindness of unfaithfulness, blinding them on this point so that they can neither hope nor believe in the true God. Thus, like a viper, he bites all the Holiness and Honor of God through these people who follow him at his instigation and who, in everything, scorn the living God through their unfaithfulness. Indeed, they do not uphold according to the true faith the true God, who is invisible, nor likewise the soul, the spirit of man. For all their affection inclines toward things that are carnal, and this is why they trample underfoot everything that comes from God, just like the one who seduced them, for, scorning the words of Truth, they glory in lies and in false doctrine.

The fallen angel indeed knows by his intellect that intelligent man has the possibility to do what he wants. And he had recognized this in the first man who had accepted the order from God. And so, just as he deceived the woman, he strives to destroy in these people what God had ordered, namely that they increase and multiply, by suggesting to them that they live not according to the precept of the Law, but according to what they decide for themselves at the devil's suggestion.

Hence their relentlessness in mortifying the body, in fasting, all for rejecting God's precepts and the normal order of procreation.

Hildegard urges the rulers of the city to expel these people:

Therefore, listen carefully to this, you kings, dukes and princes and other Christian people who fear God, and drive these people from the Church by depriving them of their liberties, by banishing them and not by killing them. For they are images of God. May the spirit of fire who is the living source penetrate you by his grace so that you might do this before God's day of wrath, in order that neither honor nor the bliss of body and soul will be lacking to you.

". . . by banishing them and not by killing them"— religious as well as civil authorities would have reason to remember Hildegard's advice! The nun attributes to original sin the failure of the body that dies and the fact that man is deprived of the vision of the true light. And it is to the rulers whom Christ has given us that it falls to "watch so that people, before their death, can be purified of all guilt; because of this, they themselves should have pure hearts so as to stay watchful and never to judge except according to the judgment of almighty God." And she issues a warning regarding respect for poverty and for the poor themselves for the love of Christ: "Although God allows the rich to possess their wealth and be able to support the poor, nevertheless it is the image of the poor man which is his own image, and which he loves."

Hildegard decidedly appears to have had foreknowledge of those religious who would, in the steps of Friar Francis and Saint Dominic, give preferred place to Lady Poverty, undertake the reformation of customs, and renew monastic life in order to combat the heresy, or rather the sect, of the Manichaeans.

CHAPTER IX

THE LAST STRUGGLES
AND SACRED MUSIC

AFTER HER SOJOURN IN Cologne, Hildegard would make two more preaching journeys, one to Mainz, the other in the province of Swabia, undoubtedly during the year 1170. We do not know exactly what were the stages of this final journey, which she undertook when she had surpassed the age of seventy; at the very least, in that highly picturesque region, bristling with towers and castles, riddled with underground caverns, she stopped at Kircheim unter Teck, which preserves a twelfth-century church dedicated to Saint Martin. The clergy of that city, in the person of Werner, abbot or provost of the community of local parishes, wrote her to ask pressingly of her for the text of the sermon that she had delivered to them (letter 52 of the Patrology).

He calls her "mother and spouse of the Lamb," and the tone of his request clearly shows the state of mind in which he addresses the visionary:

Since the perfume of your virtues has penetrated the vast reaches of the earth, as your heart has enhanced the world by opening it to the good, yet also by prophesying the future and by enabling through the grace of the Holy Spirit the contemplation of heavenly things, we find it to be a worthy thing, even though we are unworthy, to commend ourselves to your holiness as to your brotherly love. [This is why they allow themselves to ask of her] that in your maternal piety you not neglect to write and pass on to us the words that, with the Holy Spirit instructing you in our own presence and that of many others in Kircheim, you preached to us on the subject of negligence that priests have in celebrating the divine sacrifice, so that these words might not be erased from our memory, but that we might have them under our eyes, drawing our attention from now on.

Sabina Flanagan, in the excellent study she did on Hildegard's correspondence, seems surprised by the reaction of this brotherhood of priests, whom the nun harshly called back to a more zealous piety and who, although weak-willed in comparison to her, are keen to preserve the remembrance of her exhortations. Yet this is to mistake the state of mind of a community that could have passed through phases of halfheartedness without thereby losing sight of their early fervor, and who, touched by Hildegard's exhortations, felt regenerated by her. The image that Hildegard had presented to them was in itself exalting; she recalls it in her letter of response, which is distinguished by the detail of being dated, with the year 1170:

I saw, while awake in body and soul, a very beautiful image, having the form of a woman of the finest sweetness and so lovable for her delightful beauty that the human spirit could not conceive it; her stature reached from the earth up to heaven. Her face was extremely bright, and her eyes looked up to heaven. She was dressed in a very white robe of shiny silk, and she wore a mantle adorned with extremely precious stones, emeralds, sapphires, diamonds and pearls, and on her feet had shoes of onyx. However, her face was covered with dust and her garment on the right side had been torn and her mantle had lost its elegant beauty, her shoes had also been soiled, and she herself cried out to the heights of heaven in a strong and ominous voice, saying: "Listen, heaven, for my face has become dirty, and weep, O earth, for my garment has been torn. And you, abysses, groan, for my shoes are filthy. The foxes have their dens, and the birds of the sky have their nests, but I have neither helper nor comforter nor staff on which I could lean and that could support me."

She spoke again: "I have lived in the heart of the Father until the Son of man, who was conceived and born of a Virgin, shed his blood, he who married me and endowed me with this same blood to regenerate me, by the pure and simple regeneration of the Spirit and of water, from what the serpent's hatred had contaminated and wasted. Those who watch over me, namely priests who should make my face shine like the sun and thanks to whom my garment should shine like lightning and my mantle sparkle with precious stones, and my shoes glow with whiteness, have cast dust on my face, have torn my garment, have dirtied my mantle and soiled my shoes. They who should have adorned me in every way have ravaged me in everything. [The vision continues by enumerating the insults done to her by the very ones who should have contributed to her beauty.] The priests of Christ who should have made me pure and should have served me in purity do nothing but aggravate these wounds in their excesses of avarice by running from one church to another."

Hildegard then denounces the effects of this criminal avarice:

Some false priests, to be sure, deceive themselves in wanting to have the honor of the priestly office without carrying out its responsibility. This cannot be, for no one will be given recompense unless the appropriate work has been done. Ever since the grace of God has touched man, it has led him to work so that he might receive recompense for it.

Hildegard's era was not yet the one in which ecclesiastical benefices would be distributed widely to titleholders who would have no care for carrying out the related duties; this would be the case in the fourteenth and fifteenth centuries, or again in the classic epoch, when the monarch would find himself enabled by the concordat of 1516 to appoint bishops and monastery abbots. Yet accepting the revenues of these benefices intended to remunerate an ecclesiastical position without much concern for the position itself represents a human—too human!—tendency which has always existed. Hildegard seems to have been aware that the greed of temporal princes, as well as the wrath of the people, would not fail to take effect some day against those priests inclined to make money out of their position:

Princes and people, reckless, are going to turn against you, O priests who until now have neglected me. They will chase you and put you to flight, and will carry off your riches because you have not been attentive to your priestly office in its time. And they will say about you: "We reject the Church with its adulterers, its abductors, its people filled with evil." And in doing so they will wish to render service to God, for they say that the Church is polluted by you. . . . By God's permission, many people will begin to be upset with you in their judgment, and many will nurture erroneous thoughts in your regard when they see that you count as nothing your priestly office and your consecration. They will help the kings of the earth to throw you out and to covet your earthly goods; and the leaders who will rule you will gather to decide to banish you beyond their borders, because you have chased from your midst the innocent Lamb by your very wicked works. [And Hildegard affirms that she has heard in her vision a voice coming from heaven:] This image is that of the Church.

And the vision continues:

Again I, poor woman, saw this female form holding a sword out of its sheath, suspended in the air, of which one side of the blade was turned toward heaven and the other toward the ground. And this sword was extended over the spiritual people whom the prophet of old had foreseen when with admiration he said: "Who are they who fly like clouds and like doves over the windows?" They indeed, lifted from the earth and separated from the common run of people, should live in a holy manner with the simplicity of doves both in habits and in works. At present, they are depraved in their habits and works.

Thus the vision concludes on a reassuring note, for she had seen enough that lived in priests stamped with purity and simplicity, and that God looked on, as at the time that he answered the prophet Elijah "that there were still seven thousand men in Israel whose knees had not bowed down to Baal."

At this time, may the inextinguishable fire of the Holy Spirit fill you, so that you might convert to the best way.

The sermon pronounced at Kircheim seems to have nourished in detail this powerful image, which the letter written in response to the request of the priests of the district describes. A severe warning, yes, supported by a grand evocation, which seems to have yielded its fruit since the listeners were bent upon seeing the text with their own eyes.

We can suppose that during her journey in Swabia, Hildegard also made her way to the abbey of Hirsau, not far from Freudenstadt, which in its time was one of the most renowned Benedictine abbeys. Founded in the eleventh century, it adopted the Cluny reform, and more than one hundred monasteries were affiliated with it. Nothing remains of it today except for the Eulenturm (owl tower), a beautiful square tower from the beginning of the twelfth century, which stood in the cloister facing the church; its first floor, once the abbey library, contains the rare vestiges that remain of the whole edifice. The memory of Conrad of Hirsau is connected with this library; a near contemporary of Hildegard, he spread and taught appreciation for the classic authors of antiquity, such as Cicero, Horace, and Ovid, all sources of culture that, according to him, monks ought to study in order to develop in themselves a taste for beauty, refinement of expression, and literary sense.

We should return, however, to the preceding journey of Hildegard, which she made in the direction of Mainz, for it is connected with the difficulties that overshadowed the last years of her existence, and which also stirred her to write some remarkable pages, especially on music.

Her letter to the city's prelates covers the whole story:

In a vision . . . I saw myself obligated to write about what was enjoined upon us by our rulers [Hildegard and her convent were dependent on the archdiocese of Mainz] on the matter of a dead man who was buried among us under the direction of a priest, without any difficulties thereby arising. Some days after he was buried, our rulers ordered us to withdraw him from our cemetery. Thus, struck by terror as one can imagine, I looked as usual toward the true light and I saw this in my soul, with my eyes open: that if, in accordance with their order, this dead man's body were to be withdrawn, this rejection would bring great danger down upon us, under the form of a vast blackness over the place where we are, surrounding us as a black cloud, of the kind that normally appears before for a thunderstorm. So, with regard to the body of the dead man, who had confessed, been anointed, received communion and has been buried without contradiction, we would not have wanted to withdraw him, and we did not submit to the injunctions of those who tried to persuade or to order us to do so; not that we spurn in any case the counsel of just men or of our prelates, but lest we seem to do injury, by some sort of female cruelty, to the one who, when he was still alive, had received the sacraments of Christ. Nevertheless, in order not to keep ourselves entirely in disobedience, we halted the canticles of divine praise, according to the interdict placed upon us, and we abstained from receiving the Body of the Lord; while by custom we would receive it about once a month,[8] we abstained from it. Concerning this, while both my sisters and I conceived great bitterness over it, and were left in great distress, afflicted by a great weight, I heard these words in a vision: "It is not on account of human words that it is fitting

---

[8] Let us recall that in those times Mass was daily, even for many lay people, while communion was relatively rare; it was always given under the two species of bread and wine, up till the middle of the thirteenth century.

for you to abstain from the sacrament that my Word has put on, and who is your salvation and who was born virginally of the Virgin Mary, but for that you must ask the permission of your prelates who have cast this interdict on you." . . . And so, I heard during this same vision that I was guilty of not having come into the presence of my rulers in all humility and devotion to ask them for permission to receive communion, especially given that having accepted this dead man could not be imputed to us as a fault; he was buried after having been fortified by his priest with everything that befits a Christian, and was accompanied by the usual procession to Bingen without anyone finding reason to object.

To understand this passage, it is necessary to recall that an excommunicate, one who is "cut off from the communion of believers," evidently has no right to religious burial; yet on this point the prelates of Mainz seem to have been poorly informed, since, Hildegard states, the deceased had precisely been reconciled with the Church before dying. Nevertheless, whether a misunderstanding or stubbornness on the prelates' part, the monastery where there was a refusal to obey had been placed under interdict, namely that the Eucharist could not be celebrated there, and that the psalms and hymns of the monastic day could no longer be sung, but only recited in low tones. This clause must have distressed Hildegard, for whom music was a vital element, especially in the life of a community and in the expression of its piety. Thus she set about to develop in her letter to the clergy of Mainz a magnificent statement in praise of music. She writes:

> Let us recall, that humans have wished to recover the voice of the Living Spirit that Adam had lost by disobedience, he who, before his fault, while still innocent, had a voice similar to that which the angels possess by their spiritual nature. . . . This resemblance to the angelic voice, which he had in Paradise, Adam lost and, in this art with which he had been endowed before the sin, he fell asleep at that point that, waking as if from a sleep from what he had seen in a dream, he became ignorant and uncertain after having been deceived by the devil's instigation. And, by opposing the will of his Creator, he found himself wrapped in the darkness of inner ignorance by his act of iniquity. But God, who preserves for the first beatitude the souls of the elect to the light of Truth, came to decide on his own that each time that he would touch the heart of certain people, in pouring upon them the prophetic Spirit, he would render to them, along with interior illumination, something of what Adam had possessed before the punishment of his disobedience.

> Then, so that man might enjoy this sweetness and the divine praise which Adam himself enjoyed before his fall, and which he could no longer remember in his exile, and to encourage man to seek them, the prophets, taught by the same Spirit that they had received, invented not only psalms and canticles, which were sung in order to increase the devotion of those who listened to them, but also invented various musical

instruments, thanks to which they emitted multiple sounds so that people could be taught interiorly not only by the forms and qualities of these same instruments, but also by the meaning of the words that they heard and that were repeated to them, awakened and practiced by these means. This is why wise and studious people, imitating the holy prophets, also found certain classes of instruments, thanks to their art, in order to be able to sing according to the soul's delight. And what they sang, thanks to the positions of their fingers and to the inflections that they used, they adapted, remembering Adam as formed by the finger of God, namely by the Holy Spirit, in whose voice every sound of harmony and every musical art, before he had sinned, was sweetness; if he had remained in the state in which he had been formed, the infirmity of mortal man could not at all have sustained the power and the sonority of his voice.

Then, when the deceitful devil learned that man, under God's inspiration, had begun to sing, and was thereby invited to recall the sweetness of the canticles of the heavenly homeland, seeing that the machinations of his trickery were reduced to nothing, he was terrified and troubled, and began to reflect and to search, according to the multiple resources of his wickedness, so that thereafter he could not only multiply evil impulses and impure thoughts or various distractions, but even in the heart of the Church, everywhere that this was possible, through dissensions and scandals or through unjust orders, to upset or hinder the celebration and the beauty of the divine praise and of spiritual hymns.

This is why [Hildegard adds,] you must reflect, you and all the prelates, with extreme vigilance and, before closing by sentence the mouth of anyone in the Church who sings the praises of God, when you suspend him, interdicting him from receiving the sacraments, all this, before doing it, you must examine with care the causes for which you do it, having first discussed it with the greatest care.

The evocation of Adam's voice, similar to that of the angels, lost with Paradise and, thanks to the inspiration of the prophets, found through singing and music, albeit with difficulty, constitutes a fascinating page in Hildegard's correspondence. She continues with this formula that is found elsewhere from her pen: "The soul is a symphony." On the same theme, she goes on to comment on the monastic hours, those times of chanted prayer that recur seven times during the day in praise of God. And just as she has already shown that the canonical hours recall the interventions of God in biblical epochs, she goes on to establish a relation between these rhythms of the day and the stages of creation:

Consider that, since the body of Jesus Christ was born of the Holy Spirit in the integrity of the Virgin Mary, so also the canticle of praise is rooted in the Church, according to the celestial harmony, by the Holy Spirit: the body is indeed the garment of the soul that has a living voice, and this is why it is fitting that the body with the soul sings with its voice the praises of God. Hence the prophetic spirit expressly commands that God be praised by playing cymbals and other musical instruments that wise and learned people have invented, for all arts useful and necessary for humans proceed from the breath of spirit that God has sent into the human body; and this is why it is right that they praise God at all times. And since upon hearing certain chants a person sometimes sighs and often groans, recalling the nature of the heavenly harmony in his soul, the prophet, considering and knowing the nature of spirit—since the soul is by nature symphonic—exhorts us in the psalm that we sing to God on the zither and that we chant on the ten-stringed lyre. . . . Thus the beginning of the day is called *lauds,* when the dawn appears before the sun and, at the same time, true wisdom and true charity, you have inspired in him a breath of life. Indeed, just as the sun after the dawn immediately sends its brilliant beams, the soul, the breath of life that is fire, of which the flame is rationality, makes itself known by the knowledge of Good and of Evil—just as the sun is known by its splendor.

The following time during which God placed Adam in Paradise and showed him the glorious pleasure of that Paradise, allowing him every fruit except the tree of the knowledge of Good and of Evil, was the time from prime until terce.

The time during which Adam called by their names everything that breathes and all winged creatures of the sky that he saw and knew in the vision of his knowledge, and during which he heard God speak to him in the brightness of his divinity, was the interval from the hour of terce until sext; God then appeared to him on the eastern side, yet he did not see his Face, but rather the brilliance of his Face. Then God, having gladdened him with this knowledge, sent sleep over him and thus, with his soul glad in the wish for sleep, he fell asleep like a son before his father. In this sleep, God kept his spirit at the same level as the body where he had sent him with knowledge of Good and of Evil, and everything that was to come. He showed him it, namely his progeny destined to fill the heavenly Jerusalem. And, in this same sleep, he removed a rib from him and made the woman from it; when she was led to him and he saw her, she greatly gladdened Adam. He and his wife thought about what they were going to eat and to do; she waited for her husband while standing near the tree of Good and Evil. Seeing this, the ancient serpent, who was looking at her as the angels look at the Lord, approached her in order to deceive her. The interval of time during which this occurred was as the interval between sext and none.

The woman whom God had made in Paradise from a rib of the quickened man—while by foreknowledge he foresaw the life by which all life prevails when it descends into the woman through whom man is destined to enter into the glory of the heavenly Paradise—seduced by the serpent, offered to her husband deadly food. When they found themselves naked in their own light, the light of God that had first appeared to Adam appeared to them as a flame from the southern side and said: "Adam, where are you?" This interval of time was as the period between the hour of none and that of vespers. After this, once they were banished from Paradise, they came into the world and there found night over the earth.

This commentary on the canonical hours, and the magnificent evocation of musical art preceding it, bring to mind the passage of the seventh vision, in *The Book of Divine Works,* in which Hildegard evokes "the flute of holiness, the zither of praise, the organ of humility which is the queen of virtues." Thus, for her, the instruments are by nature dedicated to "the praise of God" as the hours marked in the course of the day in prayer and the singing of psalms. She brings to light a profound agreement between the rhythms of time and of the liturgy, that could not be fully understood except in her era when the quest of reasoning was not so much in demonstration as in analogy: it is indeed a whole play of symbols that for her thus conveys the monastic life.

Given this, she vehemently admonishes "those who impose silence on the canticles of God's praise without any sure reason for doing so." She states: "They who have unjustly deprived God on earth of the beauty of his praise will not enjoy in heaven the company of angelic praises, unless they correct themselves in this through true penance and humble reparation." The prelates of Mainz should not have been insensitive to such reproaches, since they could take pride in a magnificent tradition in the realm of liturgical chant: One of their archbishops, Rhabanus Maurus, is given credit for the famous hymn "*Veni Creator Spiritus.*"

And the *Dom* of Saint Martin, the cathedral of Mainz—the oldest of the great Romanesque churches of Germany, together with the one in Speyer—evokes, with its double choir, the splendors of liturgical chant which in Hildegard's age allowed two choirs, each situated in an apse, to answer each other, filling the vast edifice with their voices. Its millenial anniversary was celebrated in 1975, after the wounds of time had been repaired; the whole remains worthy of the historical importance of a cathedral whose archbishop had been prince elector and archchancellor of the Holy Roman Empire.

Hildegard's plea was convincing. The dispute with the prelates of Mainz would not, however, be resolved for some time; they seemed to have raised numerous reservations to her appeal. Still, she was helped by Philip, the archbishop of Cologne. He went personally to Mainz, bringing with him a knight who affirmed that he had been absolved from the excommunication that he had incurred at the same time as the man buried at Rupertsberg. The same priest who had absolved them both seems to have been present. The interdict thus would be lifted, to the immense relief of the religious gathered around Hildegard.

Then a misunderstanding cropped up: the archbishop of Mainz, Christian, then absent because he was staying in Rome, sent a letter confirming the interdict of which the nuns of Bingen were victims. Hildegard wrote to him (letter 8), recapitulating the whole affair and begging him to take notice of the conditions in which the excommunicate, whose burial was causing so much trouble, had been reconciled with the Church a year before his death. She insisted so effectively, "imploring your mercy with tears and supplications," and appealing to the testimony of the bishop of Cologne, that finally she moved Christian, archbishop of Mainz, to write a second letter. Now better-informed, he also declared himself more inclined to compassion since the nuns' innocence now appeared more evident to him. He concluded by referring to his earlier ignorance on the exact conditions of the disputed burial, and asked "pardon and mercy" for it. The misunderstanding, which circumstances had prolonged far beyond reason, was finally over.

The letter to the prelates of Mainz also contains, besides the passages concerning the Cathars, a broad elaboration on the sacrament of the Eucharist and the priestly ministry. Indeed, this letter contains all kinds of riches, the same that we find presented in Hildegard's visions, but here in a more accessible formulation. Thus we can cite a familiar thought of hers as it relates to the soul, "the greenness of the body":

The soul indeed works through the body and the body through the soul, and the soul is the greenness of the body, and so man is fully revealed, in whom fire, water and watery air—or humid air—are found, that humid air within which one breathes in and breathes out the humid breath. Indeed, just as the sun, from the point on the circle that it completes with the restless wind, spreads the heat of its rays and stirs up all its powers and virtues, so also the rational soul in the body spreads its humid breath, and this enables the creature to know thanks to its reason. To be sure, the soul and the body with their powers and their particular resources, as well as the flesh and the blood, are but one, and by the three, namely body, soul and reason, a human is complete and can work.

A bit earlier, before this explanatory passage on man, she expresses this sentiment on human beauty that is common in her epoch:

The person is happy indeed whom God has made as the tabernacle of his wisdom, thanks to the sensuality of his five senses who until the end of his life through the sound desires of good works, the hunger of justice and the sweetest virtues that cannot tire him, ascends continually from newness to newness by the grace of God, and so he will happily reach the glory of the life that does not change, which has no distaste and remains ever without end. Indeed, just as God makes all things new until the very last day, and what he wills to do after that last day, thanks to his power and his infinite possibilities, remains known to him alone. Meanwhile, those blessed humans who were living in this newness will have, thanks to the zithers and the symphonies and in the sound of all praise, a joy of all joys without end in God's presence.

In the same letter, there is a beautiful passage on the poor, in which she says she is inspired by the Letter of Saint James.

The rich man is honored because of his great wealth; he is welcomed, he is honored, especially because of the aid that he brings against adversity and in fear of his power. The poor man should be welcomed for the love of Christ and because he is a brother of the man. The one and the other cannot be considered as alike, because that would show no discernment. If anyone were to seat the rich man and the poor man together, the rich man would spurn it and the poor man would be alarmed. But the poor man should be welcomed and considered for the love of God, because he is a brother of the man; and although God allows the rich man to possess wealth and that he share it with the poor, nevertheless he loves the figure of the poor man who is his image. Indeed the rich man, because of the pride of his wealth, commands people whom he could harm, and he treats them as if they were not human in the same form as himself; in this way the name of man is blasphemed, man who by himself is the image and likeness of God.

Finally, this long letter ends with a prayer in which Hildegard invokes in particular "Holy Mary, star of the sea." She portrays the Son of God

as a good and wise gardener, picking good and perfect herbs for everyone's use, namely good and perfect people who have been like the good herb in the good soil, since they have listened to him and, by listening to his words, they themselves have gladly obeyed his precepts in faith and charity.

With every conflict settled, Hildegard passed her final year in the monastery of Eibingen, where she was assisted by the monk Wibert of Gembloux, Volmar's successor. Unfortunately he did not leave us any account of the abbess's death; for this we can only refer to the text of the *Life*. Its writers refer back to the accounts by the nuns who were around Hildegard. "The blessed Mother," they write,

had piously fought for the Lord in many struggles and works. Seized by distaste for this present life, she desired every day to escape from it and to be with Christ. God, granting her desire, revealed her end to her as she had wished until then in the spirit of prophecy, and she foretold it ahead of time to her sisters. Finally, suffering in her infirmity, she passed happily from this age to the heavenly Bridegroom in the eighty-second year of her age, on the fifteenth of the calends of October (September 17) in the year 1179. Her daughters, for whom she was their joy and consolation, took part amid bitter tears in the funeral rites for their beloved mother, for although they had no doubt about the compensation and help that she would bring to them, nevertheless, because of the departure of her by whom they had always been consoled, they felt in their hearts immense regret.

Then there is a description of the wonder that took place afterward:

Above the house where the holy virgin gave up her blessed soul to God, at the beginning of Sunday night, two very brilliant arcs of diverse colors appeared in the sky, which proceeded to widen out to the breadth of a large disk extending over the four corners of the earth, from north to south, the other from east to west. At the summit, the two arcs joined: a bright light emerged, like that of the lunar circle, which, spreading far off, seemed to drive away from her house the shadows of the night. In this light, a gleaming cross was seen, at first small, then growing little by little, becoming immense; around it were displayed innumerable circles of various colors, in which could be seen little crosses shining in their circles, smaller than the first one. And when the first one extended itself in the firmament, it spread especially toward the east, and shone on the ground around the dwelling in which the holy virgin had passed from earth to heaven, and then seemed to wane. One can believe that through this sign God showed what brightness he had showered upon her whom he loved in the heavenly dwellings.

The *Life* mentions next some miracles occurring at the tomb: some healings as well as "a sweet odor coming from her tomb."

Hildegard died in a time of full blooming. Romanesque art still attested its vitality, and the Gothic vault easily fit in, enabling planning for ever larger and brighter naves. And a multitude of spires were going to point to the sky, ever higher, just as poems of daring lyricism.

Activity expanded everywhere; this was no longer the collective spirit within which the nun's birth occurred, yet pilgrimage to the Holy Land, with all that it entailed, increased. Nonetheless a terrible blow befell Christendom with the loss of Jerusalem, recaptured by Saladin only eight years after Hildegard's death. The Holy City was lost, but not the Holy Land; around Saint John of Acre, reconquered with much effort, there gathered combatants, residents, and religious orders, templars and Hospitallers. Around them, the population changed somewhat: merchants were always and everywhere to be found in the tracks of pilgrims, but their presence became persistent and their action decisive. Venice did not take long to assert itself in the Near East as the splendors of Byzantium declined, before they were wrongfully pillaged and apportioned among the very armies that had intended to come to the aid of Christendom, and became used as auxiliaries by big Mediterranean commerce. As the visionary's predictions were realized in Languedoc, wars and upheavals followed one another just at the time that the Manichaean temptation would be overcome by gentleness and sound doctrine. Yet a threat of another kind would soon become evident with the birth of the Inquisition, and all the perversions contained in power by the appeal from the spiritual authority to the temporal authority—which would not take long to turn back on the very ones who had invoked it.

The approaching times would not be lacking in mystics nor in visionaries, stimulating that continual need for reform and conversion that the Church has, just as every living person. One can nonetheless remark that in this there would be little of the quality of Hildegard, who was both immersed in her age and utterly faithful to the Gospel. If we compare her visions and her sermons to those of Joachim of Fiore, her near contemporary (he died a quarter century after her, in 1204), we find in the latter a renewed apocalyptic power, the accent placed on prophetism, much more than the visionary from the banks of the Rhine had done—yet we also find disturbing elements of deviation. The Calabrian monk would go so far as to predict the coming of a new era, the reign of the Spirit—even then, a kind of "New Age"!—and his predictions would attract many of those whom Franciscan fervor ought to have preserved from similar errors. He would certainly have a long "spiritual posterity," about which Cardinal de Lubac has drawn our consideration: all those who have predicted "a third age to come in time and on this earth, which would be the age of the Spirit." He adds that "this posterity is constantly in metamorphosis, and not just within or on the margin of Churches, but even in the laicized thought of modern times"; indeed, his visions were linked to all the millenarianisms to come. In some way Joachim had taken the baton from Merlin and the Sibyls. This was an error that Hildegard had never fallen into.

Furthermore, on another level altogether, enthusiasm would grow in the intellectual world for an Aristotelianism that, at the University of Paris—which, as is known, was formed at the beginning of the thirteenth century—would become dominant and entrenched, from definitions to syllogisms. Aristotle was for the scholarly world of that time what Hegel would become for that of the nineteenth and twentieth centuries. Now, the university claimed to hold "the key of Christianity." They pushed this too far when the popes came to place themselves under the protection and influence of the kings of France during the "Avignon exile" in the fourteenth century. In the meantime, a remarkable synthesis was certainly elaborated between Aristotelian reasoning and Christian faith thanks to Saint Thomas Aquinas, hence a philosophy that would impose itself with time, but no longer open, as formerly, on a universe in continual creation. It would not take long to reach the notion of a closed universe, in which all parts could be unraveled by rational analysis—something that was not at all doubted in the era of Berthelot.

Meanwhile, the gap grew; mystical life and social life followed parallel ways. Far from any crowd, behind high walls, the paths of perfection were followed in the shelter of ever stricter cloisters, in the reformed orders such as those of Carmel. In the clergy, the hierarchy—which was appointed by the temporal power in France after the Concordat of Boulogne in 1516—was tending to a kind of austere autonomy. Since the end of the thirteenth century, in the very architecture of the Church, one could notice the image of an isolation between clergy and people, even in the celebration of the eucharistic mystery: the choir limit, marked off by a grill or tapestry, becomes a stone wall in the cathedral of Albi. It is significant that the part most richly sculpted and painted is the interior while, for the use of the people, the rood screen is erected as well as the pulpit for solemn preaching. It is true that, since the end of the eighteenth century, a movement in the other direction is discernible that asserts itself little by little.

Thus, various phases follow upon one another and intersect in the course of the Church's life. Our age seems to experience some kind of spiritual hunger which does not believe it can find its food in parish life. A personage like Hildegard, a kind of prophet, a "mouth of God," who cries out what the living Light inspires in her, is perfectly integrated into her times: corresponding with the emperor as well as with the pope, influential on the political level as well as on the spiritual level, turning her gaze toward the humblest plants as well as toward infinite space, she could doubtlessly help in this reconciliation of different orders of thought, of different aspects of life, for which there seems to be a longing today.

APPENDIX

OVERVIEW OF HILDEGARD'S POETIC AND MUSICAL WORK

IT SEEMED WORTHWHILE to us to conclude this work with some texts giving an idea of the poetry of Hildegard, and thus of her musical work, so important, since in her time music was not separated from poetry.

The reader will find here some specimens of her activity in this field, which can be complemented by disks and cassettes also available. We have limited ourselves to three poems, the best-known ones—*Hymn to the Holy Spirit, Hymn to Saint Mary,* and *The Sequence of Saint Maximin*—mentioned in the preceding pages.

But above all, we were eager to give a translation of the thirteenth vision of the *Scivias*. This vision has a special attraction: it contains the theme, and, as it were, the substrate of the *Ordo Virtutum*. It is the strangest poetic and musical work of the nun, since it is actually a kind of opera. In it are seen the Virtues, personified; the devil, the faithful soul that he tries to corrupt; Humility and Charity who defend her; etc. The whole theme of this *Ordo Virtutum* is laid out here; it is therefore the birth of a musical project under the pen of the one composing it: a germinal work, in progress. It has seemed important, indeed captivating, to us from this point of view.

We hope that the reader will find the same interest in it.

The *Scivias*
"Vision 13"

I saw then a very luminous air, in which I heard about the meanings of every thing that had been wondrously said, diverse kinds of music in praise of those who live in heavenly joys, who persevere courageously on the path of truth, and in the laments of those who are remote from these same praises of joy, and for exhorting the virtues of those who take courage for the salvation of the peoples and who resist the devil's wiles. But the virtues themselves rebuff these wiles, so that faithful people pass finally from sin to the supreme joys through penance. And this chant, like the voice of a multitude composing a harmonious symphony in the praises of those who have been lifted above by stages, was saying: O gem among the most splendid, the serene honor of the sun is instilled in you, source coming from the heart of the Father, you who are the sole Word through whom he created the prime matter of the world, which troubled Eve; this Word made the human in you; you are the shining gem from which the Word himself has drawn all the virtues, just as in prime matter he produced all creatures. O you, sweet branch, flowering from the stem of Jesse, how great is the virtue that the divinity perceived in its very beautiful daughter, just as the eagle fixes his gaze on the sun, when the Father most high contemplated the brightness of the Virgin when he willed that his Word be made flesh in her. For in a mystical mystery of God the spirit of the Virgin was touched, and wondrously a bright flower sprang up in this same Virgin. And he said again: O glorious living Light, angels who gaze in burning desire upon the divinity, the divine eyes in the mystical darkness of every creature, with which you can never become weary! O how greatly does your image rejoice in glorious joy, she who is in you pure from every evil work, which happened first in your companion, the lost angel who wished to fly above the hidden sanctuary of God. Thus it happened that he, rejected, fell into ruin, but everything that was done by the finger of God had the effect that his instruments [would be] occasions of suggestion on his part.

For you, angels who guard the peoples, whose beauty shines on your faces, and you, archangels who welcome the souls of the just, and you, Virtues, Powers, Principalities, Dominations and Thrones[9] who are counted in the number of five secrets, and you, cherubim and seraphim, seal of God's secrets, praise be to you who gaze at its source upon the jewel box of the ancient choir. Indeed, you see the interior power of the Father that arises from this choir as a face. And he said: O you, remarkable humans who penetrate, by looking with the eyes of the spirit, what is hidden, and announce in the luminous shadow the piercing and living light budding on this branch which alone flowered at the arrival of this light taking root; you, holy people from the past who had foretold the salvations of exiled souls who were as if immersed in death, you who have turned around as wheels, speaking admirably of the

[9] Names of the five angelic powers.

mysteries of the mountain that touches the sky, crossing many waters where it is anointed at the moment when among you the shining light appears that illumines, from the start, the mountain itself. O you, happy roots through whom was planted the work of miracles and not the work of crimes through the twisting path of the diaphanous shadow! And you, O deep voice of fire surpassing the polished stone of the threshold of the abyss, rejoice in your head. Rejoice in him whom many have not seen on earth, who had ardently called him with their prayers. And again, it was said: O burning cohort of flowers of a branch without thorns, you who are the music of the globe of the earth, surrounding the regions of sense in folly, feeding among the pigs, which you have rejected by the instilled help of him who planted the root in the tabernacle of the entire work of the Word of the Father, you who are the noble race of the Savior penetrating the way of regeneration of water thanks to the lamb who sent you, sword in hand among the cruel dogs, who destroyed his glory in the works of his fingers, making clear that it was not made in the submission of their hands, among which they did not find it. For, O luminous band of apostles, emerging in the true knowledge and opening the enclosure of the Devil's mastery, washing the captives in a fountain of living water, you are the bright light in the black darkness, you support like a strong row of columns the bride of the Lamb in all her adornment, and for his glory she is mother and Virgin and carries his standard. The Lamb is indeed the spotless bridegroom, and his bride is spotless.

She then said: O triumphant victors, who in the shedding of your blood have saved the building of the Church and have entered through the blood of the Lamb, nourishing yourselves with the slaughtered calf! What a great reward you will have, for you have disregarded your body while alive, imitating the Lamb of God, in praising his suffering, into which he has brought you in order to restore those who are his heirs. You, rosebuds who in the shedding of your blood are blessed and you rejoice with the greatest joys, weeping and exuding that which you receive that comes from the inner spirit of counsel dwelling in him before the age, when nothing had been established, honor be from the beginning of your company: you who are the instrument of the Church and who in the wounds of your blood have cast abundant dew on them.

And again, she said: O successors of the courageous lion, ruling between the temple and the altar in his service, like the angels who resound with praises and who at the same time are near and ready to help the peoples, you are among those who do this, having always the concerns of the Lamb in their duties. O you, imitators of the lofty person in his precious and glorious significance, your raiment has been grand ever since the soul has gone forth liberating and giving refuge in God to the idle and to pilgrims, or also making them black and white and relieving them of heavy burdens. For you have the duties of the angelic order and you know in advance the most important foundations, where they should be set, hence your honor is great. And, also, she said: O you faces of beauty who gaze at God and build in his dawn. O happy virgins, you are noble, you in whom the king considers himself, since he has already placed in you all heavenly adornment, and therefore you are the sweet garden in which you breathe out the perfume on all adornment. O noble greenness who shine in the sun and who gleam in candid serenity on the orbit that confines none of the most remarkable earthly beauties: You are encircled by the embraces of the divine mysteries. You are red like the dawn and you shine like the flame of the sun. And again this sound resonated like the voice of the multitude longing to return to the same level in harmony, it lamented, saying: O weeping voice, that of very great pain. Ah! An admirable victory has arisen in the admirable desire of God; in this is secretly hidden the delight of the flesh. Alas! Alas! There where the will has not known fault, and where human desire has fled cowardice, there are very few of those who come to you: weep, weep then in innocence for these, you who have not lost your integrity or simple modesty, and that the greed of the serpent's mouth could not devour, for it is with great neglect that humans listen to you. O living font! Great is the sweetness in you that has not lost the face of these; but you have seen clearly beforehand that you will shield them from the fall of the Angel, those who believed they could have what it is not permitted to keep. This is why: rejoice, daughter of Zion, for God gives you many of those whom the serpent wished to take away from you and who, at present, shine with a greater light than the one that would have been theirs earlier. Indeed, the living light says of them: I have fooled the devious serpent in what he instigated, which was not as convincing as he himself thought.

This is why I have sworn by myself that in these causes I have done more and still more than in those. O serpent, your joy must leave you, for I have removed something of your incitement: what you have never found in your cruelty, O maker of illusions in all shame.

Now, this tumult, as the voice of the multitude hearing the exhortation of the virtues for the help of humans and in contradiction to those who undergo the attacks of diabolical tricks, the virtues dominating the vices, and humans finally returning to penance through divine inspiration, this voice in all harmony cried out: "We are the virtues in God, and in God we remain: we struggle for the King of kings and we separate Evil from Good; for we have appeared in the first combat where we were victorious: when that one collapsed, who had wanted to fly above himself; this is why at present we struggle, coming to the aid of those who call upon us, and trampling underfoot diabolical tricks and leading toward the dwellings of bliss those who wish to imitate us."

Laments of souls clothed in the flesh. We, we are pilgrims. What are we doing, turning ourselves toward sin? We should be daughters of the king, but we have fallen into the darkness of sin; O living sun, carry us on your shoulders, toward the just heritage that we have lost in Adam. O King of kings, we fight in your combat.

Invocation of the faithful soul. O sweet divinity, O gentle life in which I will wear a magnificent garment, receiving the one whom I lost in the first appearance. I yearn for you, and I call upon all the Virtues.

Response of the Virtues. O blessed soul, sweet creature of God, who have been lifted up into the lofty grandeur of the wisdom of God, you love deeply.

The faithful soul. Oh, I will gladly come toward you so that you might give me the kiss of the heart.

The Virtues. We must fight along with you, O daughter of the king.

The faithful soul. O harsh pain and heavy weight that I bear in the garment of this life—for it is very hard for me to fight against the flesh.

The Virtues. O soul! Constituted according to the will of God, O blessed instrument, why are you so weak against what God has defeated in virginal nature? In us you should rule over the devil.

The faithful soul. Help me, so that with your support I can stand firm.

(*The Knowledge of God intervenes.*)

The Knowledge of God. See what there is of that with which you are clothed, daughter of salvation, and be steady, and you will never fall.

The faithful soul. Oh! I do not know what to do, and where should I flee? Woe is me, I cannot come, I cannot perfectly fill what I am clothed with. Surely I am going to reject him.

The Virtues. O unhappy conscience, O wretched soul, why do you hide your face before your Creator?

The Knowledge of God. You do not know, you do not see, you do not taste him who created you.

The faithful soul. God has created the world. I will not offend him if I wish to make use of it.

(*The Devil intervenes.*)

The Devil. Fool, fool! What use is it for you to suffer? Look at the world, and it will embrace you with much honor.

The Virtues. Alas! Alas! We virtues weep and we lament, for God's sheep is about to flee life.

(*Humility intervenes.*)

Humility. I am Humility, the queen of the Virtues. I say: come to me, all you Virtues, and I will feed you so that you might learn to look for the lost drachma, and that you might crown her, happy in her perseverance.

The Virtues. O glorious Queen! O sweet mediatrix, we gladly come.

Humility. This is why, O chosen daughters, I keep you in the royal chamber. O daughters of Israel, God has supported you under the tree, so that in this time you might remember that it has been planted. Rejoice then, daughters of Zion!

The Devil. What then is this power, that not one of them is outside of God? I say: anyone who wants something from me and will follow my will, I will give him everything. But you, with your followers, you have nothing that you can give, for you yourself do not know what you are.

Humility. With my companions, I know very well that you are the ancient dragon who wanted to fly above the heights, but God himself has cast you into the depths of the abyss.

The Virtues. As for all of us, we dwell in the heights.

The faithful soul. O you, royal Virtues, you are beautiful and resplendent, in the light of the great sun, and your dwelling is sweet! This is why there is woe for me, since I am far from you.

The Virtues. O fugitive, come, come to us, and God will welcome you.

The faithful soul. Ah! Ah! Great delectation as drawn me into sin. This is why I no longer dare approach you.

The Virtues. Do not fear, do not flee, for the Good Shepherd seeks in you his lost sheep.

The faithful soul. I need now for you to receive me, for I reek with my wounds, with which the ancient serpent has contaminated me.

The Virtues. Run toward us, and flee those tracks into which you will never fall in our company. And God will heal you.

The faithful soul. I am the sinner who has fled life and I will come to you full of wounds, so that you will offer me the shield of redemption.

The Virtues. O fugitive soul, be strong and put on the armor of light.

The faithful soul. O you, the entire company of the queen of virtues, and you, white lily with the crimson rose, turn toward me, for I have wanted to flee to you as a pilgrim, and help me so that I can rise again in the blood of the Son of God. O true medicine that you are, Humility, give me help, for pride has wounded me with many vices and has injured me with deep scars. Now I flee to you, and so deign to receive me.

Humility. O you, all you Virtues, take in the sinner who laments her scars because of the wounds of Christ, and lead her to me.

The Virtues. We want to lead you; we do not want to leave you, and the whole heavenly host rejoices over you. Thus, it is normal for us to burst into symphony.

Humility. O unhappy daughter, I want to embrace you, for the great physician has suffered harsh and bitter wounds for you.

The Devil. Who is she or where does she come from? You have embraced me and I have drawn you away from there, and now you forget me by going back. I am going to strike you down in combat with you.

The faithful soul. I have learned that all your ways are wicked, and this is why I have fled you. And now, O deceiver, I am fighting against you!

The faithful soul (again). On that account, most high Humility, help me, help me with your medicine.

Humility. O Victory who have vanquished this same being in heaven, hurry with your companions and come to bind the devil.

(*Victory addresses the Virtues.*) O courageous and glorious combatants, come and help me defeat this liar.

The Virtues. O sweet combatant in the source of the stream that swept away the rapacious wolf, O you, glorious crowned army, we gladly fight along with you against the deceiver of souls.

Humility. Bind him then, O magnificent Virtues!

The Virtues. O our queen, we shall obey you and fulfill your precepts in everything.

Victory. Rejoice, my companions, for the ancient serpent is bound.

The Virtues. Praise to you, O Christ, king of angels, O God, who you are, you who have had in yourself this great decision by which you destroyed the infernal thirst among the publicans and sinners who today shine in supreme goodness; this is why, O king, praise be to you. O almighty Father, from you flows the source with outstanding fervor; lead your children into the steady wind of sails and waters, so that we may lead them to the heavenly Jerusalem. And these voices were like the voice of a multitude, as when the multitude lifts its voices high. And the sound reached me so that I could understand them immediately without difficulty. And I heard a voice coming from this same luminous air, saying to me: Praise should be given to the supreme Creator with an incessant voice from the heart and from the mouth; for he himself has gathered not only those who remain standing and upright, but also those who fall and bend in the higher seats by his grace. From this you see, O human, this extremely luminous air: designating the simplicity of the joy of the dwellers on high, in which I hear in all the preceding senses, in the admirable expression of different kinds of music, in praises of citizens on high, in their joy, of those who persevere courageously in the way of truth, and in the laments of those who have been called to the praises of the same joys; for just as the air comprises and sustains everything under the sky, so you hear in all the marvels which have been spoken of, that have been shown to you by God, a sweet and gentle symphony that resonates with the joy of those who have been chosen in the heavenly city and who persist in sweet devotion toward God; and in the laments of those whom the ancient serpent seeks to ruin them and take them back, but whom the divine Virtue has nonetheless courageously led to the society of blessed joys: pronouncing in them these mysteries which are unknown to the human spirits bent toward the ground; and in the exhortation of the virtues of those who take courage in the salvation of peoples thanks to which they repel diabolical tricks; but these Virtues themselves restrain them, so that faithful people finally pass from sin to the supreme joys through penance; for here the Virtues in the spirits of the faithful enable them to resist vices so as to atone for them, thanks to which they resist the diabolical breath; but people cast into sin which they have surmounted with a power of the most courageous return on a divine sign to penance, when they seek out and lament their faults of the past and when they examine and take guard over what will follow it.

This is why this sound, like the voice of a multitude unfolding in harmonious symphony in the praises of the highest levels, for the symphony leads to unanimity and to concord, repeats the glory and honor of the inhabitants of heaven, so that it cries out loudly what the Word says openly. Thus the Word designates the body; the symphony manifests the Spirit, since it proclaims the divinity in a celestial harmony and since the Word presents the humanity of the Son of God. And since the power of God, flying everywhere, comprises everything, so that nothing makes the least obstacle to it, so human rationality acquires great power for singing in a loud voice and to arouse in the symphony sleepy souls to watchfulness. This is what David shows in the symphony of its prophecy, and Jeremiah displays it in the plaintive voice of his laments. So also, O human, who are by nature poor and fragile, listen in the symphony to the sound of inflamed ardor of virginal modesty, in the caresses of the words of the flowering branch, and the sound of the loftiness of the living lights who shine in the city on high, and the sound of prophecy of profound words, and the sound of the expansion of the apostolate in admirable terms, and the sound of those who have offered themselves faithfully even to the shedding of their blood, and the sound of the secrets of the priestly office, and the sound of the virginal enthusiasm of those who flourish in a vigor come from on high since the creature faithful to the supreme Creator expresses itself in a voice of exultation and of joy, and often repeats to him its thanksgiving. But you also hear this sound, this chant like the voice of the multitude resounding in the laments of those who have come back to these same levels in harmony, for the symphony rejoices not only in the unanimity of exultation in those who courageously persevere on the right way, but also in the accord of the return to the way of justice by those who had strayed, and finally it exults at the true bliss of those who are upright, since the Good Shepherd himself has led with joy to the flock the sheep that was lost.

This is why, as you listen to it, this sound like the voice of the multitude cries out in its harmony for the exhortation of Virtues coming to the aid of the human, and in the objection of those who move away from diabolical tricks to the virtues that overcome vices and to the people finally returning under divine inspiration to penance; for it is a sweet embrace in these virtues that draws faithful people toward true bliss, yet it is also a cruel offense against the vices of diabolical tricks; but the result is that the virtues utterly weaken these vices, and for those who consent to it, they draw them with the help of the supreme aid toward an eternal reward through true penance, in the way that has been shown to you in these voices of harmony.

For the symphony softens hard hearts; and it brings them a savor of sweetness, and calls down upon them the Holy Spirit. Hence these voices that you hear are like the voice of the multitude when this multitude raises its voices very high; for the praises of jubilation borne in the simplicity of charity and of unanimity bring the faithful to this unanimity where there is no more discord, since they make those who are placed on earth yearn by heart and by mouth for the supreme reward. And the sound of these passes through you, and you hear it without any difficulty or delay; when divine grace has acted, it will carry away all darkness and all shadow, making pure and luminous everything obscure in the carnal senses owing to the weakness of the flesh.

This is why whoever understands God faithfully offers incessant and faithful praises, and is jubilant continually in faithful devotion, in the same way that David my servant, led by me in a spirit of depth and of height, exhorts, saying: "Praise him at the sound of the trumpet, praise him on lyre and harp, praise him on drum and horn, praise him with strings and organ, praise him with resounding cymbals, praise him with jubilant cymbals, let every spirit praise the Lord" [Ps 150]. This means: you who know God with simple intention and pure devotion, adore him and love him: praise him in the sound of the trumpet, that is, in a sense of rationality, for the lost Angel having fallen while bringing with him those who consent to perdition, in contrast the band of blessed spirits will persevere in the truth in a reasonable way. And they have cleaved to God in faithful love. Praise him on the lyre of deep devotion and on the harp of singing delicious as honey, for the sound of the trumpet is followed by that of the lyre, and the singing of the lyre is followed by that of the harp, just as the blessed angels who persevere in the love of the truth have awakened among created humans some prophets with admirable voices: they whom the apostles followed with the sweetest words. And praise him on the drum of mortification and in the choir of exultation, for after the harp comes the drum, after the drum, the choir exults, just like the apostles when they preach the words of salvation: the martyrs who for God's honor have borne in their bodies different tortures have lifted up among themselves true doctors of the priestly office. Praise him on the strings of human redemption and on the organ of divine protection since in an exulting choir the voices of the strings and the organ appear as true scholars in the office showing the truth of bliss: the virgins come forward, who had loved the Son of God true man as on the strings, and have adored the true God as on the organ, because they have recognized him and have believed in him as true man and true God. What does this signify? That when the Son of God put on flesh for the salvation of humans, he did not lose the glory of divinity. Hence the blessed virgins, choosing him for their bridegroom, true man in betrothal and true God in chastity, have taken him in faithful devotion. Yet, furthermore, praise him on well-resounding cymbals: this means in those accents which in true joy make an outstanding sound, when people, lying deep in their faults, touched by divine inspiration toward the supreme height, stand up straight out of this bottom. And praise him in the cymbals of jubilation, which means in the accents of divine praise, where powerful virtues very courageously achieve victory and destroy vices in people, and lead them through ardent desire toward the happiness of true reward when they persevere in the good. Thus every spirit of goodwill, for believing in God and for honoring him, praise the Lord, namely him who is the Lord of all, for it is right that one who desires life should glorify him who is life.

And, again, I heard a voice arising from the luminous air, saying: O most high king! praise to you who do all this in a simple and uneducated person. Yet again the voice cried out from heaven with a strong shout, saying: Listen and pay attention, all you who wish for reward and bliss. O you, humans with a believing heart who await the supreme recompense, welcome these words, place them within your heart, and do not refuse this warning when you come to visit me. For I am the one who proves the truth, God living and true, and, not keeping silent, I say and repeat again: Who could prevail against me? Whoever will try this, I will reject him. Thus man does not fear the mountain that he cannot move, but he dwells in the valley of humility. But who can travel paths without water? The one who refreshes himself in the whirlpool and who divides the fruits without eating. And my tabernacle, how and where will it be? My tabernacle, my tent, is here where the Holy Spirit spreads his refreshment. What then? I am there in the middle. How? The one who approaches me worthily will fall neither on high nor into the depths, nor across. How so? Because I am that charity which neither haughty pride nor sharp blows drive back and which the host of evils does not confine. This is why I cannot build at the height of the sun's footstool. Courageous are those who show their courage in the valleys, they scorn me; dazed, they reject me at the sound of whirlpools; wise, they take my food, and each one readies a tower for himself according to his own will. But I will confound them with the small and the weak, just as I hurled Goliath back thanks to a child, and as I overcame Holophernes through the person of Judith. This is why if anyone refuses these mystical words of this book, I will hold my bow over him and I will pierce him with arrows drawn from my quiver, and I will knock the crown from his head, and I will make him like those who fell at Horeb when they had murmured against me. And whoever will have uttered any curse against this prophecy, the same curse that Isaac uttered will come upon him; and the one who embraces it and keeps it in his heart and follows right ways by it will be filled with the blessing of heavenly dew. And the one who tastes it and places it in his memory will become a mountain of myrrh, incense and all spices, and will be filled with many blessings, climbing from blessing to blessing like Abraham, the newly adopted new bride of the Lamb, will embrace him like a pillar under God's gaze; and the shadow of the Lord's hand will protect her. But if anyone has rashly hidden these words from the finger of God, or weakened them by his folly, or set them aside in some strange place by reason of human concern, and so scoffs at them, he will be reproached and the finger of God will stop him. Then praise, praise God, O happy womb, in all the miracles that God has established in the imprecise form of the appearance that arises, that he has seen in advance in the first appearance of the rib of the man whom God drew from the mud. He who has the sharp ears of interior sense, in the ardent love of my likeness will aspire to these words and will inscribe them in the conscience of his spirit. Amen. Amen.

Three Poems by Hildegard
The Sequence of Saint Maximin

The dove has seen
Through the slits of the shutter,
Where, before her face,
The balm emitted the fragrace
Of splendid Maximin.

The warmth of the sun arose,
And shone in the darkness
Where the gem arose
For the building of the temple
Of the blessed's pure heart.

This lofty tower
Built with the wood
Of Lebanon and of cypress,
Adorned with hyacinth and diamond,
A city excelling in the arts
Of all the artists gathered.

He has run, a fast deer
Toward the source of purest water
Flowing from the highest rock

That irrigated the two bushes
Of spices.

O you, perfume master,
Who are in the greenness
So sweet of the king's gardens,
Climbing toward the heights
When you perform
The holy sacrifice
Among your gathered sheep.

Among you shines the architect
Temple wall
Who desired eagle's wings
Kissing nursing Wisdom
In the Church's glorious fruitfulness.

O Maximin
You are the mountain and the valley
On the one and in the other a tall building
From which the elephant and capricorn come out
And where Wisdom took her delight.

You are strong
And gentle
Among the rites and the choirs exalting the altar
Climbing like spice fumes
Toward the pillar of praise.

Where you intercede for the people
Who lean toward the mirror of light
Of whom praise is spoken out loud.

Hymn to Saint Mary

Hail, O greenest branch
Who sway in the windy breeze
Of the prayers of the saints.

When the time came
That you flowered in your branches
Hail, hail to you
Whom the sun's warmth stirred
Like a balm's perfume.

For on you bloomed the lovely flower
That gave perfume to all aromas
Left dry until then.

And everything then appeared
In full greenness
And the skies shed their dew on the grain
And the whole earth was gladdened by it
For its bowels brought forth
Their wheat
And the birds of the sky
There found their nest.

Then it became people's food
And the great joy of banquets
Thus, O sweet Virgin
No joy is lacking to you.

All that Eve spurned
Let it today be praise to the Most High.

Hymn to the Holy Spirit

O fire of the protecting Spirit
Life of the life of every creature
You are holy, giving life to every form.

You are holy
You who anoint the wounded in peril
You are holy
You who cleanse
Reeking wounds.

O you who breathe in holiness
And the fire of love
O taste of sweetness in the breast
Infusion of hearts
In the good odor of the virtues.

O purest source
In which is contemplated
That God attracts strangers
And seeks lost souls.

O armor of life and hope of protection
Of all the members
O girdle of decency
Save the blessed.

Guard those
Who were imprisoned by the enemy
And free those in chains whom your divine power wills to
save.

O path of the bravest
Who have penetrated everything
In the heights and on the ground
And in all abysses
You bring them together and assemble them all.

From you flow clouds
The ether flies
The stones become wet
The waters flow in streams
And the soil exudes greenness.

You always lead the learned
By the inspiration of wisdom
And make them joyful.

Then praise be to you
Who resound with praise

And joy of life,
The most lively hope and honor
Giving the rewards of light.